Praise for *Mind Reading for Managers* and Kim Seeling Smith

Mind Reading for Managers is a refreshing and effective approach to people management. The 5 **FOCUSed** Conversations have guided our line managers to apply more structure and direction to their conversations but without overtaking their own personal management style. The framework is flexible and we have applied it to our Induction program plus our regular one-on-one huddles with our employees.

Madel Giles, HR Advisor
Razorfish Australia

Since the course I have found that I have been able to apply more structure to the conversations I have with my team — not just the content of the conversations, but also the themes of the conversations. There has certainly been an improvement in process that assists my team in expressing themselves on a number of specific subjects in an open but structured way. This has provided me with greater insight into their motivations and what they value most in their working environment. As a result — since taking the course my one-on-one meetings have become more relevant, and I regularly receive positive feedback from my staff telling me that they look forward to my catch-ups with them.

Marcus Babajews, Head of Development
Razorfish Australia

The leadership within my organization found the results [of the Employee Retention Diagnostic Survey] to be so potent that we asked Kim to present her analysis to the leading 30 stakeholders of our business. She is a consummate professional who delivers on her promise.

ick Bensted, Manager
le & Business Services
CBP Lawyers

D0916545

The *Mind Reading for Managers* program is helping us develop world class and consistent managerial skills across our divisions. Although the program gives you a step-by-step framework and a number of different exercises you can use with your staff, it also allows managers the flexibility to use the tools as they wish, in whatever manner works best for them. The main outcome of the session was to ensure that they hold monthly one-on-ones with each of their staff and cover the five must-have conversations, regardless of whether they followed the program to the tee or modified it to suit their own needs and style. I am pleased to report a definite improvement in the conversations between managers and staff — with many managers taking advantage of these tools in each conversation.

Kim Kirsten, Senior Executive
HR & Business Services
Commonwealth Superannuation Corporation

Kim has delivered several training courses to our management team. On each occasion the feedback received has been fantastic, with the course exceeding expectations. Ignite's training is both informative and engaging, inspiring participants to utilize the tools and techniques presented. Kim is an exceptional presenter who is impressive in her delivery and shares a wealth of knowledge within her field of expertise.

Daniela Burton, Human Resources Advisor
CARDNO

Working with Kim Seeling Smith and Ignite Global has been a real eye opener for me. They have reinforced the concept of how important people are to any business. Understanding those working alongside you is key to any good operator. I believe that I personally, as well as our business, have really benefited from this program.

German Romo, Principal
Northrop Consulting Engineers

Kim…is one of the finest recruiting professionals I have ever seen. She has a rare blend of commitment, skill, passion, and knowledge.

Chandan Ohri, Director
KPMG

The quality of your employee engagement survey is excellent and equal to anything I have seen in the market. However, it is your commitment, professionalism, and passion that was far beyond my expectations and what made the experience such a positive one for all. You have established an excellent rapport with the Foodco team, so much so that they think of you as one of the staff!

Serge Infanti, Managing Director
Foodco Pty, Ltd (Muffin Break, Jamaica Blue, Dreamy Donuts)

Kim delivered an exceptional plenary session at our annual Risk Retreat conference this year — it was one of the highlights of the entire conference. Her presentation was extremely engaging, informative, and practical with a suite of tools the advisers could take back to their businesses to implement right away. We highly recommend her as a brilliant presenter and subject matter expert on the topic of employee engagement.

Olivia Romano, Technical Support Manager
Risk Specialist Network|MLC & Nab Wealth

Kim is a straight shooter who will open your eyes to the recruiting mistakes you have been making for so long!

Megan Motto, CEO
Consult Australia

I first met Kim at an IT Recruitment and Retention Forum and was impressed with her presentation, which I found highly engaging and very informative. I later engaged Kim on a project to help revamp our talent management website due to her industry knowledge and understanding of the talent attraction, hiring and retention lifecycle. Kim has a lot of passion and enthusiasm for what she does, so it's been a pleasure to work with her.

Sue Tu, Program Manager
Cisco Systems

I would encourage candidates and employers to consult with Kim on your next important career or recruitment decision.

Craig Richardson, Chief Financial Officer
Coca Cola Amatil, Auckland, New Zealand

Having worked within some of the biggest recruitment firms in the world, which includes over 300 consultants, I would confidently advocate that Kim is certainly one of the best consultants I have had the pleasure of working with. Kim's commitment to client/customer service is second to none, she not only meets their expectations but exceeds them. I have no hesitation to recommending Kim to anyone that is interested in progressing their career.

Christian Gordon, Consultant
Aequalis Consulting

Kim was a fantastic keynote speaker at SMF Australia's LEADit 12 conference. The message she brought to us was spot on! Our audience really resonated with her 5C's for Employee Engagement and Retention. I hope to have the opportunity to work with her again.

Bradley Busch, Operational Risk Manager
Macquarie Group Limited

As a professional speaker who focuses on the world of recruiting, selecting and hiring top talent I have spent the last 20 years building a knowledge base and honing my speaking skills. Over those 20+ years I have heard hundreds of other speakers speak on the same subject. Kim was one of the very best I have ever heard. She offers great insight in to today's challenges facing recruiters, hiring managers, and applicants. More importantly, she offers tools and techniques to help overcome those challenges in a most professional and entertaining way.

Mel Kleiman, CSP, President
Humetrics

We've hired Kim to speak on a number of regional APAC webinars to our HR and Business Management audiences — her topics have drawn huge response and attendances, and her interactive presentation style has driven excellent feedback — so much so that my colleagues in the U.S. and U.K. have now started recruiting her to speak on their webinars too!

James New, Marketing Principal
Citrix Online

My team recently brought Kim Seeling Smith in from Ignite Global to do her *Mind Reading for Managers* workshop. The workshop was outstanding! The 5 **FOCUSed** Conversation tools I learned from the workshop changed the way I communicate with my staff in a positive way. Overall, she has made a difference in my life at work, and for that, I am thankful for her services and mentorship.

Elia Twigg, Public Works Director
City of Palm Bay, Florida

MIND READING
FOR MANAGERS

*5 FOCUSed
Conversations
for Greater
Employee Engagement
and Productivity*

KIM SEELING SMITH
FOUNDER AND CEO, IGNITE GLOBAL

IGNITE GLOBAL LICENSING PTY LTD.

Contents

Acknowledgments

This book is about conversations. And it began as a conversation. A few years ago, Joris Luijke and I both spoke at an HR conference in Australia. Joris is currently the VP of People at Squarespace in New York, but at that time he was the VP HR & Talent at Atlassian, a highly successful Sydney-based software company recognized for their innovative HR strategies. Joris and I instantly connected and began to meet from time to time to share ideas. One of our conversations (neither of us can remember exactly which one) sparked the idea for a program to help managers communicate better with their staff. Thank you Joris. I only hope that our brainstorming sessions were half as valuable to you as they were to me.

This program eventually became *Mind Reading for Managers.* I say "eventually" because, like most programs of its kind, it's gone through many iterations and revisions. The current content and format are due in large part to those clients — especially those early adopters — who trusted me enough to take these concepts out for a spin and allowed me to adapt and revise as I taught and they implemented.

Chief amongst these early adopters are Jamie Shelton, the Sydney Regional Manager for Northrop Consulting Engineers, and his Section Leaders. It's been a privilege to work with this group of bright engineers who have always been willing to stretch beyond their comfort zones and approach managing and leading people very differently than they had in the past. The last three years have been an amazing journey. Thank you all!

Early adopters or not, I am extremely grateful to all of our Ignite Global clients over the last five years, too numerous to name. They are large companies and small, public and private sector, based in the U.S., Australia, New Zealand and further afield. Many of their stories appear in this book. All of them remain in my heart.

I would also like to thank Jerry Mooketsi, Bec Thrift and Maddie Benjamin of the Toowoomba Regional Council for asking a simple question one day, "Could you do a 'Train the Trainer' and allow us to deliver this content ourselves?" The answer, of course, was yes and that event directly led to the writing of this book.

To develop the facilitators guide for the "Train the Trainer" I engaged the services of Catherine Mattiske and Mel Barn of The Performance Company. I've worked with many service providers of all types in the past, but rarely have I received as much value for the dollars I've spent with them.

And it was Catherine who, after looking at my "Mt. Everest of content" told me, "You have a book here." Indeed I did. Thank you for seeing it and encouraging me to finally sit down and write it.

Thank you too, to Vicki St. George of Just Write, editor extraordinaire. I don't know if Vicki is clairvoyant, but she sure channeled me! She helped me fill in some missing bits, round out the chapters and helped me (literally) dot my i's and cross my t's. Thank you for making this process much easier!

Most of the actual writing of the book was done at my friends Deb and Mark Bennett's Dallas townhouse. They are the type of friends with whom I have an open invitation to stay, regardless of whether or not they are home. Unluckily for me I didn't get to see them during the time I was writing, but luckily for me I had the house to myself with no distractions and I was able to finally see this project through.

But I have another reason to thank Deb Bennett. When I graduated from The Ohio State University I worked as a CPA and Management Consultant with KPMG. I was not a good accountant, but it took me five years (and several jobs) to realize that. At that time, Deb was a Regional Manager for the staffing firm, Robert Half International. I had known Deb for several years and we both served as Board members for the American Women's Society of CPAs. I called her one day expressing my realization that I needed to figure out what I really wanted to do when I grew up. She replied by saying, "I've waited four years to have this discussion with you! You want to become a recruiter!"

After some convincing, I decided she might be right and I embarked on a 15-year journey with Robert Half, Hudson Executive Search, and two small, boutique firms that proved to be my most impactful and enjoyable professional experiences before launching Ignite Global. I learned so much about what staff need to be happy and productive and what companies do to encourage (or block) that engagement and productivity. Those lessons became not only the basis of all of the work that we do at Ignite but also my mission in life.

I had some wonderful mentors during my time in recruiting, including my dear friend Peggy Page. I think about you often and miss you dearly.

In fact, I've had some extraordinary mentors throughout my life and career. I was fortunate to have an exceptional education and to be taught by some truly gifted, compassionate and innovative teachers including: English teacher Mary Jo (Dahlquist) Newburg who taught me the value of the written word, Chemistry teacher Ludwig Kroner who taught me that I could go on when I didn't think it was possible, and band directors David Reul and the irrepressible Alden J. (Buz) Hoefer, who both gave me too much to mention in the confines of a few pages. Mr. Hoefer, I am proud to be part of your opus.

I have also been blessed with a robust personal support system and I'd like to thank a few now.

To my friend and colleague Lynne Schinella of Ripe Learning for keeping me sane from time to time and keeping it real all of the time.

To my lifelong friends Patty (Wellman) Rohwer, Betsy (Binney) Gruba and Vanessa (Fouch) Marks. There are no friends quite as dear as old friends.

And to my family. To my mother and father, Lin and Don Seeling, who helped to shape me into the person I am today — I hope I've made you proud. To my grandfather, George Jung: Grandpa, you were always a role model and gave me a real sense of who I wanted to be in the world. You also instilled in me my work ethic and the motto that you always lived by and that I've adopted as my own, "Where there's a will, there's a way." If it weren't for that belief, this book wouldn't have been written. And to my uncle and aunt, Jim and Norma Jung, who were always there for me.

Finally, I would like to thank my partner in life, David Toyne. Your unwavering love, support and belief in me are my greatest blessings in life and have kept me going on days when it would have been much easier to quit. Building a business is hard work. Sharing a message I truly believe in and am passionate about is lonely and exhausting sometimes. Having you in my life has made it not only far less lonely, but filled with love, adventure and fun. Thank you for not taking no for an answer.

Kim Seeling Smith
Oconomowoc, WI
July 2014

P.S. Yes, Oconomowoc is a real place! It's my hometown and although I moved away in 1978, I happened to be here when I finished the last words of my first book — these acknowledgments. That to me is as it should be.

Introduction

Why Managers Need to Read Minds

To win in the marketplace you must first win in the workplace.

Doug Conant, CEO of Campbell's Soup

I've been a management consultant and recruitment and retention specialist for over 20 years. As the founder of Ignite Global, a company specializing in innovative solutions for the Social Age, I've spoken to companies and on stages around the world on the subject of employee selection and engagement.

A few years ago, I was asked to speak at a Rewards and Remuneration conference in New Zealand. They wanted me to talk about how rewards and remuneration could help companies increase their employee engagement levels.

I said, "Sorry — I'm probably not the right person for your conference."

There was a long silence on the other end of the phone, then one word: "Why?"

"Because I believe that the best way to engage and retain staff lies outside of the compensation and benefits area," I told them. "We're in a new age of business now — I call this the Social Age, where innovation, creativity and strategic thinking is critical in your employees. And the best way to engage and retain Social Age employees is to *make sure you hire the right people and then talk to them about the right things frequently enough to make a difference.*"

The good news is that the conference organizer called me back and said they wanted me to speak about building employee engagement in this new age.

But the bad news is that far too many businesses still believe that the best way to find, retain and get the most from their employees is with the old "carrot and stick" approach.

You've undoubtedly seen (or maybe even used) this reward-and-punishment style of motivation: give employees performance incentives while you threaten them with job loss if they don't pull their weight. In this model, most of a manager's coaching and interaction with staff consists of perfunctory performance reviews every six to twelve months — conversations that managers and employees find extraordinarily unhelpful and stressful at the same time.

This "old-school model" is broken and we need to fix it so we can better engage our staffs and create the healthy work environments where both people and companies not only survive but thrive. But there's no time to waste. Not only are demographics stacked against us — with the disparity between the number of Baby Boomers retiring and Gen Y's (and beyond) entering the workforce — but we are also in the midst of a critical skills shortage brought about by the shift from the Industrial Age (characterized by routine, tactical and predictable work) through the Information Age and into the Social Age (characterized by having to be more innovative, strategic and creative).

Employee recruitment and retention is shaping up to be THE issue of the next decade.

Fortunately, most employee engagement (and many performance management) problems can be solved through effective communication. Yet most managers don't talk to their staff enough, don't know what to talk with them about or how to talk to them effectively. They don't understand what truly motivates their employees or how to increase engagement at work.

This new Social Age demands a revolution in the ways we attract, engage and manage our staffs. To truly increase employee engagement, managers must communicate with their teams about the factors that drive engagement. (I call these factors *Currencies of Choice* because they have much more power to drive and engage than pay and benefits.) Managers need to have the *right conversations frequently,* with the *right people,* in the *right way.*

I created the *5 FOCUSed* Conversations to help managers talk directly with their teams about the five most important elements that make the biggest difference in productivity and emotional "buy-in" at work. These conversations have been the foundation for the *Mind Reading for Managers* course I've taught successfully throughout Australia, New Zealand, Asia and the U.S., and I'm now sharing them with you in this book.

The *5 FOCUSed* Conversations described in *Mind Reading for Managers* are designed to plumb the depths of your employees' minds to learn about their true goals, aspirations, strengths and motivations. They also provide a very effective performance management tool and a way to gather honest feedback from your staff. While this model won't teach you how to have tough conversations with non-performers, it will significantly reduce the need for those conversations by better managing performance and proactively addressing what your staff want and need to succeed.

I wrote *Mind Reading for Managers* not as a management book, although applying this framework will certainly help you better manage staff. Nor did I intend it as a leadership book, although talking with your staff about what engages them will lead the way to a healthier work environment. My goal is to help managers have the kind of conversations with their staff that will ignite their potential and create a more high-performing as well as enjoyable work environment.

The tagline for my business is *Light Up Your Workforce*® because that's what I believe we need to do in this new Social Age of business. I want to help people to have careers that they absolutely love — because life is too short to spend eight hours a day (or more) five days a week (or more) doing something you dislike or actively hate. I want managers and employees to be fully engaged in the work they do, to feel good about themselves, to marshal all of their resources and realize all of their gifts in pursuit of fulfilling lives and careers.

And I want companies to build healthy work environments by using Social Age Engagement Solutions™ to attract, engage and retain the right staff to maintain a competitive edge in today's global economy while creating a healthier, happier, more engaged and productive workforce.

To increase employee engagement, you don't really have to read the minds of your staff; nor will it take a lot of time or effort on your part. All it takes is five conversations, delivered consistently and with a focus on discovering the specific elements that will light up each member of your staff. And when you help to ignite your team's potential, you'll find your own engagement, productivity, satisfaction and success "blazing" as well.

1 The Employee Engagement Crisis

*This is just a job.... If this were my career,
I'd have to throw myself in front of a train.*

Jim Halpert, *The Office* television show

The war for talent is over, and talent has won.

Yes, today the number of workers required to run a business is smaller than ever, but the available pool of workers is shrinking. As Baby Boomers retire, there are fewer Gen X and Gen Y (also known as Millennial) workers to take their place. According to the U.S. Bureau of Labor Statistics, by the year 2020 only 16.2 percent of the population will be between the prime working ages of 35 to 45 years old.[1]

And it's not just demographics driving the talent war: there is a growing skills shortage as well. We are now automating and/or outsourcing the most mundane, repetitive tasks, freeing our staff to do more innovative, strategic or solutions-oriented work. But it's getting harder to find and retain workers with the skills, abilities and attitudes needed for those more complex jobs. Indeed, a 2007 survey by the McKinsey Global Research Institute discovered that 47 percent of executives surveyed believed that, of all global trends, the intensifying competition for talent would have the most significant impact on their companies in the future.[2]

"Talent has become more important than capital, strategy, or R&D," stated Ed Michaels, a director of McKinsey Company and co-author of *The War For Talent*. "People are the prime source of competitive advantage."[3] Organizations that don't recognize talent's victory and significantly change the way they hire and manage staff will lose the very talent they need to not only survive, but to thrive in today's economic landscape. Market share, corporate status, reputation and organizational sustainability are all in danger.

Today's leaders must become experts in managing human capital. As someone who helps companies build healthy work environments by using innovative approaches to hire and manage staff, I have worked closely with managers and HR professionals for over 20 years. Based on my research and experience, I devised a five-step system for companies to be able to (1) hire correctly, (2) classify and manage appropriately, (3) compensate fairly, (4) motivate, recognize, and reward effectively, and (5) communicate clearly with both current and future employees.

The Cost of Hiring and Retention

People are not your most important asset. The right people are.
—**Jim Collins**

As every corporate executive knows, hiring an employee is just the first step. Even when you do everything right during the hiring process, you may still be surprised once the employee comes on board. The superstar you hired may end up "flaming out," or worse, being a drag on the rest of your staff. Team dynamics or changing personal circumstances can affect individual behavior and performance.

Unfortunately, replacing an employee can be difficult and expensive. Turnover costs — to "off-board" a current employee and hire a replacement — can range between 90 and 200 percent of the employee's annual salary, depending on the position.[4] For example, a 500-person organization with an average salary of $80,000 and just 10 percent annual turnover will spend approximately $3 million per year in replacement costs — a significant amount of money off the bottom line. And that cost doesn't factor in "lost time" as the employee mentally "checks out" before leaving. Nor does it include the "opportunity cost" of the one to two years it can take for a new hire to get up to speed.

And it's not just tangible value lost when staff depart. According to economists Kevin A. Hassett and Robert J. Shapiro in their study of intellectual capital in the U.S., the total value of "intangible assets" (including intellectual capital and employee "economic competency") in the American economy in 2011 was worth *$14.5 trillion.*[5] So it's not surprising that many companies take incredible steps to protect their tangible assets. They spend thousands of dollars on insurance, security systems and defending their intellectual property rights.

But very few companies really understand what it takes to protect their *human* capital.

With the high price of replacing workers, it's hard to believe that many companies think that retention is just too hard in today's changing workplace. Instead of building a stable staff with enough "bench strength" to facilitate a solid succession plan, many companies are instead opting to concentrate on their recruitment process, attempting to ensure a continuous supply of new talent when their existing staff leave.

Of course, every organization should have a robust recruitment strategy, but it is no substitute for a solid structure and dynamic management processes — which will not only better engage and retain staff but also make your organization more competitive.

———•———

Many companies take incredible steps to protect their tangible assets. But very few companies really understand what it takes to protect their human capital.

———•———

Done right, however, employee retention does not have to cost a cent. In fact, the right structure and leadership processes will add to the bottom line as well as retain your top talent. For these reasons and many more, I believe that *the more effective use of resources is to maximize the effectiveness of the people who have already gone through your hiring process.* You have to get the best from the people you already employ. You need to help your people become more strategic, innovative and solutions-oriented, and at the same time help them fulfill their own personal reasons for being on the job.

In other words, you want your people to be *emotionally engaged* with their work.

The Impact of Employee Engagement (or Lack of It)

> *Employees make the decision of whether to "re-up" every day*
> *when it comes to motivation and productivity.*
> —**Deloitte University,** *2014 Human Global Capital Trends Report*

There are many definitions of employee engagement, but in essence, it's *a measure of someone's emotional attachment to their job and to the organization for which he or she works.* This emotional attachment then translates into discretionary effort. Emotional engagement usually means that the people you supervise work as a team. They are passionate about what they do and often about the company as a whole.

The good news? More and more companies are recognizing the need to keep their employees actively engaged. When Deloitte University surveyed more than 2,500 executives worldwide for their 2014 Human Global Capital Trends report, 79 percent of respondents stated that "retention and engagement" of employees was an "urgent" or "important" priority.[6]

The bad news? Studies show that current levels of employee engagement at work are staggeringly small. And the effects on productivity and profitability are equally dramatic.

Let me give you an analogy. Imagine that you walked into your office one day and found the head of IT freaking out. He told you that only 13 percent — fewer than one in six — of your organization's computers were working reliably and consistently. Another 63 percent were only sporadically reliable, sometimes "playing well" with other computers in the network but other times not, sometimes opening the wrong programs or giving incorrect information. The final 24 percent — almost one in four — were not just unreliable but actively spreading viruses throughout the system, negatively affecting the performance of all the other computers in the network.

How long do you think your business could operate with that kind of messed-up system? And yet that's exactly what most managers face when it comes to employee engagement!

According to The Gallup Organization's 2013 global survey of employee engagement, only about 13 percent of workers worldwide are *actively engaged* in their jobs.[7] Actively engaged employees consistently bring their "A-game" to work. They are motivated. They do their jobs to the best of their ability and they frequently look for ways to add value through discretionary effort and ideas.

Another 63 percent — most of the workforce — are *passively engaged*. They might do what it takes to get the job done, but they will rarely go the extra mile. Their work might be inconsistent and unreliable, causing you, their manager, to spend excessive time checking for accuracy, quality or completeness.

The final 24 percent are *actively disengaged*. They frequently exhibit performance or behavior problems. Their productivity is below average. They are disruptive to others and often their main focus is simply to keep from getting fired. Way too much of a manager's valuable time is usually spent dealing with actively disengaged employees — but such people also cost real dollars too. In a 2011 CareerBuilder survey of 6,000 professionals, 41 percent said that a "bad hire" in the last year had cost them at least $25,000; 25 percent said that it had cost at least $50,000.[8] And that doesn't even take into account the effect of one "bad apple" on your department's productivity and morale.

Gallup estimates that actively disengaged workers cost the U.S. economy between $450 billion and $550 billion each year.

Now, the "good" news is that the numbers for employee engagement in North America and Australia/New Zealand are significantly better than the worldwide average. In the United States and Canada, an average of 29 percent of workers are actively engaged in their jobs, while 54 percent are not engaged and 18 percent are actively disengaged.[9] In Australia and New Zealand, 24 percent of employees are engaged, 60 percent are not engaged, and 16 percent are actively disengaged.[10]

I put "good" in quotations because these numbers indicate that *71 percent* of workers in the U.S. and Canada, and *76 percent* of workers in Australia and New Zealand are not actively engaged in their work. To me, that's a travesty — but it's also an opportunity for you as a manager and leader.

What if you could *increase* the level of engagement of your team?

It goes without saying that you would be more effective in your job if your team is consistently doing their best work and giving their all. But have you ever stopped to consider how much more *you* might enjoy your job if your entire team was not only productive but happy too?

What if your people loved coming to work every day, they felt like they were learning, growing and developing in their roles, and that their work mattered?

What if they felt like they had the freedom to express ideas, to be innovative, creative and solutions oriented?

How much more would be possible for them and for you, both personally and professionally? After all, studies show that increased employee engagement is good for the bottom line. The Gallup Organization reported that in 2013, companies with high employee engagement levels have:

- Up to 65 percent reduction in turnover
- 48 percent fewer safety incidents
- 41 percent fewer quality incidents (defects)
- 37 percent lower absenteeism
- 21 percent higher productivity
- 10 percent higher customer ratings
- And last, but certainly not least, *22 percent higher profitability*

The truth is, your people *want* to feel actively engaged when they come to work. Why then are so many of them still disengaged from their jobs? Why aren't we doing more to fix the employee engagement crisis?

I believe that most companies just don't understand exactly how much work has changed, and the practices and processes they currently use to hire and manage people have not caught up with the new realities of what I call the new *Social Age of business*. We are in the midst of a revolution — one that will shape the workplace for years to come.

A Social Age (r)Evolution

Everything we learned in the last century about managing large corporations is in need of a serious rethink.
— **Alan Murray,** The Wall Street Journal Essential Guide to Management

Three hundred years ago work and workers went through the Industrial Revolution, where machines replaced much of manual labor but workers still performed many rote, repetitive, clearly-defined tasks with little room for creativity and innovation. By 1973, however, work had entered what sociologist Daniel Bell described as the Post-Industrial Age, characterized by non-tangible yet valuable services, largely in the areas of finance and information. It was heavily reliant on technology, innovation and creativity.

But something was missing, and, in most working environments, still is. That "something" is employee engagement.

The Social Age, which dawned in the early 21st century, used technology and globalization to free up workers' time by automating or outsourcing most mundane, repetitive tasks. The Social Age economy *demands* innovation and creativity from workers, asking them to become more strategic and solution-oriented than ever before. We now need workers who can evaluate, assess, make considered decisions and act upon them in a way that aligns with the company's goals and objectives. In fact, McKinsey says that 70 percent of new job growth will come from jobs with a high percentage of this type of work.[11]

This is why talent has won. Those capable of doing Social Age work are in high demand and can set their own terms and conditions. They vote, if not with their feet, with their heads and their hearts. And this will become increasingly obvious (and problematic) as the 21st century economy evolves.

Simply put, *the Social Age demands greater employee engagement — and it requires companies to come up with new ways to manage, motivate, and involve their workers.* "The new model will have to instill in workers the kind of drive and creativity and innovative spirit more commonly found among entrepreneurs," Alan Murray wrote in a 2010 *Wall Street Journal* article, "The End of Management."[12]

Most employees relish the thought of doing the innovative, creative and solutions-oriented work needed to compete in the Social Age over the routine, process-oriented tasks of yesteryear. And the companies that have created a Social Age workplace — like Google, Twitter, LinkedIn, The Boston Consulting Group (global business management consulting), Atlassian (software development) and Squarespace (the DIY web development company based in New York) — can be found on any number of "Best Employers" lists.

The companies that keep appearing on lists of "best places to work" can be large (Facebook) or small (Squarespace), from high-tech (like Google) or traditional industries (like Edward Jones and David Weekley Homes), from East Coast U.S. (The Boston Consulting Group) or East Coast Australia (Northrop Consulting Engineers, an engineer consulting firm with offices in Sydney, Canberra, Central Coast, and Brisbane). And the lists they appear on can come from organizations like Gallup (renowned for their workplace surveys), and *Fortune* and *Forbes* magazines, but also from online sites like Glassdoor.com, where employees directly share their opinions about their workplaces.

With all this recognition of the power of employee engagement in the Social Age, why are so many organizations still stuck in the old, Post-Industrial Age paradigm, using the same tired methods to hire, manage, and motivate their staffs? Why do organizational structures and processes continue to get in the way of employee engagement, causing frustration, unwanted employee turnover and a potentially significant impact on productivity and the bottom line?

Simple. The practices and processes that most companies use still hearken back to the Industrial Era. There has been no clear, replicable framework for creating employee engagement for the Social Age — until now.

***Mind Reading for Managers* has been written to help leaders, senior and middle managers, line supervisors and HR Practitioners increase employee engagement and productivity by communicating more effectively with their staff about exactly what the staff need to be productive and engaged in today's digitally connected, globally oriented world.**

With this model, you can learn how to plumb the depths of your employees' minds to learn about their true goals, aspirations, strengths and motivations. It also provides a very effective performance management tool (used either separately or in conjunction with the organization's own Performance Development Process) and a facility to gather honest feedback from staff members.

By using the techniques in this book, you and your organization can take advantage of the Social Age Evolution to create more engaged, happy and productive staff as well as more free time, less stress and better job satisfaction for you as a leader.

And isn't that a future everyone can look forward to?

2 "Fire Up" Your Employees with the 5 C's of Social Age Engagement™

No company, small or large, can win over the long run without energized employees who believe in the mission and understand how to achieve it.

• **Jack Welch,** former CEO of General Electric

It's 10:45 a.m. on Monday, and a reminder pops up on your computer screen or smartphone: "Meeting with Bob, 11:00 today." You sigh — this is not a meeting you're looking forward to. Bob hasn't been pulling his weight on the team and you need to talk with him about it. While you consider yourself a good manager and leader, you dislike having this kind of conversation.

You hired Bob about a year ago and thought you'd made a great choice, based on your company's usual screening practices and a couple of interviews. His skills fit the job perfectly, his references were great and he seemed eager to join the team. For the first few months as Bob settled in and got up to speed, you'd done what you could to be of help. But Bob's motivation and excitement about the job just seemed to "flatten out." Now his performance was mediocre at best. He did what was needed but wasn't really contributing to the team in the way you'd hoped. You thought you'd hired an All-Star player only to be dealing with someone whom you feel should be sent back to the minor leagues if he can't become more engaged with his work.

What do people need to be fully motivated, engaged and productive? you think.

That is a question that haunts many managers. Even the most progressive leaders — those who understand the value in treating people as individuals and who try to demystify their employees' individual drivers and motivators — can be stumped by the puzzle of what keeps workers engaged.

I believe that if we are going to hire and retain the people we need to grow our business and meet the challenges of the 21st century, we need to create a structure where they not only survive but thrive. It should be a structure that fosters the "heuristic" work that our companies need their people to do but is also the work they *want* to do. This new type of structure means that managers need to "plug in" to their employees' minds and figure out their wants, needs and desires in order to build strong, high-performing teams.

Based upon my work with hundreds of companies in the U.S., Australia, New Zealand and Asia as well as synthesizing today's most popular and relevant research, I believe that the *5 C's of Social Age Engagement*™ *will help managers unleash the Social Age competencies of innovation, strategic thinking, creativity and problem solving in the teams they lead.*

I've used this system with both individual managers and companies such as TransUnion, Northrop Consulting Engineers, Energizer, Razorfish, and many more, and they have seen dramatic increases in employee engagement, productivity, and job satisfaction. The 5 C's framework is easy to remember and not that difficult to implement. But it will require a change in your view of your responsibilities as a manager and leader, and of your actions in helping your team to perform at its best.

The process of changing the way you hire and manage people may seem daunting at first, but experience shows that taking this step by step, you can make significant changes within six to twelve months, resulting in a lifetime of more engaged, happier and more productive staff as well as more free time, less stress and better job satisfaction for yourself as a manager.

The 5 C's are as follows.

#1: Correct Hiring

Almost without exception, high-performing teams are made up of cohesive individuals who possess the same core values and work well together within the company's culture. As a hiring manager, your first job is to *determine the cultural values of your organization and hire for those.* Then you must structure the hiring process to ensure that applicants will work well within that culture.

Second, you need to *hire for competencies and strengths instead of skills and experience.* Ask yourself what strengths are required for each individual aspect of the cultural profile you developed, and then structure your interview questions accordingly.

Third, you must *develop proper interview techniques.* After interviewing thousands of candidates and debriefing tens of thousands of interviews during my 15 years as a recruiter, I can safely say that very few hiring managers interview properly. It's not their fault: after all, who teaches interview skills? But the right interview techniques are essential to getting the right hire.

This book will not touch on the first "C," Correct Hiring — that will be left for another in this series. Instead, I want to help you understand and motivate the staff you already have by using the other four C's, with particular emphasis on Communication.

#2: Classify and Manage Appropriately

Even when you do everything right during the hiring process, you may still be surprised once the employee comes on board. Team dynamics or changing personal circumstances can affect individual behavior and performance. Therefore, you must continually keep your finger on the pulse of your staff — a daunting task to many managers who either try to devote equal time and energy across the board, or who spend time with the wrong people.

The goal is to spend the greatest amount of time with the people who will give you the most "return" on your investment — the 20 percent of your team that produce the greatest results — while motivating or moving on the rest. You must classify your team correctly and provide appropriate coaching and guidance for each of the three categories of engagement. In Chapter 3 we'll talk about accurately classifying your team.

#3: Compensate Fairly

Many companies diligently strive to create attractive incentive programs in an effort to engage and retain staff. Unfortunately, these efforts actually may be counterproductive. There are several schools of thought, including the Self Determination Theory,[13] first researched and espoused by Edward Deci and Richard Ryan of the University of Rochester, which states that most individuals are far more motivated by internal or intrinsic factors than by extrinsic ones, such as pay, bonuses or benefits.

However, as Daniel Pink, author of *Drive, The Surprising Truth About What Motivates Us,* is fond of saying, "There is a mismatch between what science knows and what business does."[14] Pink cites many different research studies that conclude the same thing: incentives only produce better results when the work is *algorithmic* — replicable or repetitive tasks requiring very little creativity.

Rewards actually narrow employee focus. However, innovation, creativity, and the ability to think strategically and solve problems — the very type of work that is required from our Social Age staff — require employee focus to widen. So it seems that the very incentives designed to enhance productivity can actually have the opposite effect. *Higher pay does not necessarily equal higher productivity.*

Pay, bonuses, and even benefits should be considered hygiene factors: they have to be enough for your employees to put food on the table and to satisfy the basic human needs. But your people also need to believe they are paid fairly, consistently, and in a manner they can rely on. They also need to feel their pay is a fair trade for the value they give to an organization.

The operative word in the third C, then, isn't the "C" word at all — it's the "F" word... *fairly.*

A Compensate Fairly Case Study

In 2011 Ignite Global was asked to conduct an Employee Engagement Survey for a mid-size law firm based in Sydney, Australia. The results were outstanding. The survey painted a picture of a highly engaged workforce whose values aligned with the company's values. The staff had a very good relationship with their managers. There was a high degree of trust and respect. They appreciated a good work/life balance, felt they worked on interesting projects and were treated well.

The only wrinkle in the entire survey was around the question, "Do you feel that you are being paid fairly for the work you do?" Almost 25 percent of the staff said, "No." So, of course that point appeared in the recommendations section of the report.

Unbeknownst to Ignite however, the law firm had just conducted a benchmarking study with a large remuneration consulting organization. This study clearly showed that the firm was paying at or above market rate across the board.

Why then did the staff not feel as though they were well paid when empirical evidence showed they were? It wasn't due to long working hours (they worked significantly less than some of their competitors), nor due to stress (there were no results that indicated a high degree of stress within the firm). What was the disconnect?

The firm was able to trace this "urban myth" back to one conversation between two senior staff members. It seemed these two particular people had not received as great a pay raise as they had expected, and they had started to complain to each other about this. The complaints then extended to their direct reports, and theirs, and so on down the line.

The most shocking thing about this scenario is that the event had happened *seven years earlier!*

Because two members of staff did not get the raise they were expecting seven years ago, an urban myth had propagated throughout the entire organization that said, "Even though the firm is a great place to work with lots of flexibility, a high degree of trust and respect and the ability to do interesting work, we know that we just won't be paid as much as we would if we were working at some of our competitors." *Despite evidence to the contrary!*

When it comes to Compensating Fairly, sometimes you don't have a remuneration issue. Sometimes it's a Communication issue.

Ostensibly, organizations can accomplish this simply by paying a living wage. Many times this means paying at or a little above market rate for individual functions. But since this is a subjective assessment, companies also need to ensure that employees feel they are being adequately compensated. This can only be accomplished by managers speaking to employees, either directly or through well-constructed and independently administered employee engagement surveys.

Once people feel they are being paid adequately, studies show that they respond much better to internal motivators than they do to external ones.

And while all internal motivators are important, some are key in driving employee engagement and productivity. We will call these key internal motivators *Currencies of Choice.*

#4: Use Currencies of Choice to Motivate, Recognize, and Reward

Currencies of Choice are a result of extensive anecdotal evidence gathered by seasoned international recruiters who conducted thousands of interviews over a 15-year period in a number of countries. Thousands of people paraded into these recruiters' offices each day for over a decade and a half and told them why they were looking for another job.

This anecdotal research was then backed up by contemporary literature on the subject and supported by employee engagement studies. This research shows that Currencies of Choice — those intrinsic motivators that keep employees engaged and retained, truly unlock productivity, and unleash potential — fall into just a few areas.

Your people want to:

- Work for someone they trust and respect in a company they can support
- Work with people they like
- Be appreciated
- Have their voices and opinions respected
- Understand how to be successful in their role
- Have a career path (vertical or horizontal) that keeps them motivated and interested
- Be inspired to go the extra mile and suitably recognized and rewarded when they do
- Be able to do what they do best every day

Here are the Currencies of Choice represented in a diagram.

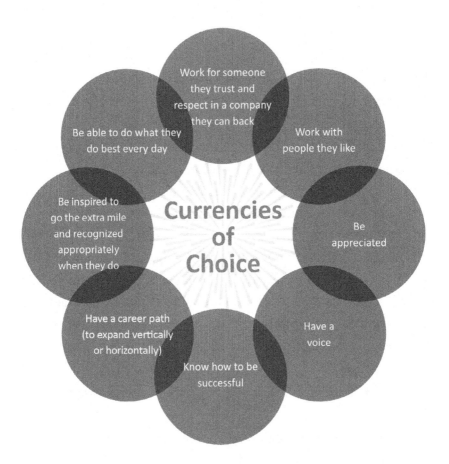

These Currencies of Choice are important to all staff, but the relative importance of each factor is dependent on the individual, his or her stage of life, other life factors and additional external circumstances.

So how do you as a manager determine which of these Currencies of Choice are your employees' *hot buttons,* so to speak?

Through conversation.

But not just any conversation: through *5 FOCUSed Conversations.* This book shows you how to use specific conversations to discover the Currencies of Choice for your people and help motivate them for greater engagement and productivity.

#5: Communicate with FOCUS

Great communication between you and your team is vital. Why?

- Robust communication is directly related to financial performance. According to a study by Towers Watson, a global professional services firm, companies that are highly effective at communication are 1.7 times as likely to outperform their peers.[15]

- Great communication is the foundation of great leadership as well as great management.

- The art of the conversation is a strong yet powerful tool which is easy to grasp and much simpler to apply than many complex management theories.

- It can also make a difference with all levels of leaders, from the newest supervisor to the most seasoned executive.

———•———

Our research confirms that effective communication is an important element of change management, and if both are done well, there is a stronger relation with financial performance. Companies highly effective at both communication and change management are 2.5 times as likely to outperform their peers as companies that are not highly effective in either area.

Towers Watson
2011-2012 Change and Communication ROI Study Report

———•———

The problem is that while most managers understand the importance of good communication, they don't talk to their staff frequently enough, don't know how to talk to them, or what to talk about. Think about it. When was the last time that you sat down in a formal meeting, one on one, to talk to one of your staff? Was it to plan or discuss an operational issue or a project? Was it to conduct their performance review? Was it to address a problem with their behavior or performance?

These are really the only culturally indoctrinated meetings we have with our people. Progressive managers might make it a point to "walk the floor" every day to catch up with staff or to catch up for a beer after work. But rarely do we as managers have *scheduled, structured conversations* with staff outside of addressing operational issues or the dreaded performance review.

And dreaded they are — by both managers and staff! Performance reviews are not only dreaded, but they are also woefully ineffective. This is primarily because they don't occur frequently enough (at best most performance review processes include quarterly catch-ups, with the vast majority requiring meetings only

---

A Few Anecdotes about Performance Reviews...

- Some years ago a human resources manager at a Silicon Valley computer company offered managers free tickets to San Francisco Giants games if they completed their subordinates' performance reviews on time.

- When David Russo headed up human resources for software maker SAS Institute, he earned employee cheers for a bonfire celebration that burned appraisal forms and ended annual reviews.

- Glenroy, Inc., a privately held manufacturing company outside of Milwaukee, burned their performance reviews in a bonfire held in their parking lot.

once or twice yearly) and because they concentrate on what is wrong about the employee rather than celebrating what they are doing well (more on that later).

Bottom line: regular, structured conversations outside of these arenas are just not part of our cultural landscape.

But there is another reason we don't talk to staff frequently enough about the things that matter, about what they need to be motivated and productive and to do their best work.

In the last 20 to 30 years, managers have been constantly asked to do more with less. This has been especially true since the Great Recession or Global Financial Crisis (depending upon which part of the world you are in). Many well-meaning managers simply don't have the time to meet with staff as often as they'd like. But, as the Towers Watson study shows, failing to do so has a direct impact on company financial performance.

So what if you were to think about communicating with your staff in terms of making an investment in the profitability and success of both you and your team?

It's like agreeing to automatically invest a certain amount from your monthly pay in a retirement account. When you first withdraw money from your paycheck, it hurts. You feel that something is missing and you have less money for yourself. But after a while it begins to feel normal. You start to "live off of" that particular monthly income. And eventually you start to see the results of making that investment. You end up with even more money, and if you've invested well, a significant increase in your assets.

The same applies to investing your time to have regular, proactive conversations about the things that matter with your staff. At first, it will feel strange, perhaps even painful. But after a period of time your entire team will come to appreciate these regular conversations as the norm — and all of you will reap the rewards of your mutual investment. You will become a more efficient and effective leader, and your team will become more capable of helping you accomplish your goals.

Hopefully by now you are convinced of the benefits of having frequent, proactive conversations with your employees about the things that matter to them, things that will help them do their jobs better and enjoy them more. Which begs the next question: what conversations will produce the best results?

I believe there are 5 *FOCUSed* Conversations managers should have with their people on a regular basis. These five conversations will help bring the dreaded Performance Management process to life, and potentially turn it from a dreaded vestige of the Industrial Age to a useful tool which accomplishes what it was meant to do: a process to help your staff become the best they can be at what they do so they effectively play their part in accomplishing team and organizational goals.

The 5 *FOCUSed* Conversations

The 5 *FOCUSed* Conversations framework is designed to learn about your employees' true goals, aspirations, strengths and motivations. They also provide a very effective performance management tool and a facility to gather honest feedback from your staff members.

FOCUS is an acronym for the topics covered in the five conversations:

- **Feedback:** Elicit open, honest feedback from staff members and give them the praise they desire (and deserve).

- **Objectives:** Craft job objectives or key performance indicator (KPI) metrics that are relevant to the company and department as well as actionable and achievable by staff members, and then hold them accountable for accomplishing those objectives.

- **Career Development:** Understand how staff members want to grow within their careers (vertically or horizontally) and how you can provide those opportunities internally instead of having them look externally.

- **Underlying Motivators:** What will drive and motivate your staff to go the extra mile, and how do they want to be recognized and rewarded for it when they do?

- **Strengths:** Help your staff understand what they are truly good at and love to do and then exploit those abilities while managing and mitigating their weaknesses for greater productivity and job satisfaction.

Let's look a little closer at each of these conversations and see how they map into the Currencies of Choice described earlier in the chapter.

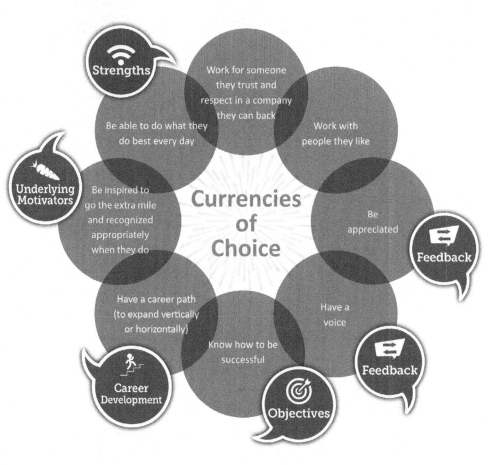

First of all, just having these conversations consistently and frequently will help your staff realize the first Currency of Choice: to work for someone they trust and respect in a company they can support. These conversations can and will also uncover any issues with the people they are working with.

Now, let's look at the rest.

F = Feedback

© iStock/alephx1

Your staff wants to be appreciated and feel that they have a voice. These two Currencies of Choice are covered in the Feedback Conversation.

Remember, the best feedback is two-way feedback. There are three types of feedback that fall under this conversation, and none of them relate to performance management (this is included in the next Feedback Conversation). They are:

1. ***Ensuring that staff are regularly updated with organizational and team information.*** Even if this information has been sent out via email, put on the company intranet or appeared on notice boards, experience shows that your staff needs to hear or read this information multiple times in multiple ways. Nothing beats one-on-one communication — even if it simply means pointing out the email, intranet page or notice board.

2. ***Giving praise where praise is due.*** Praise is a scarce commodity in many workplaces. This doesn't mean saving your praise for your monthly meetings; rather, it's a reminder to ask yourself what your people have done right in the last month and if you've

praised them for it. Even if you have, it's not a bad idea to do this again.

3. ***Giving them a voice.*** Allow them to give you open, honest feedback about what's working, what's not, and any ideas or suggestions they may have to help them do their job better, help the team or the organization as a whole. Be receptive to the feedback of those on your team. Who knows? They may just come up with a brilliant idea that makes a huge difference for you, the team or the whole company!

O = Objectives

This conversation is at the heart of performance management in most organizations.

One of the fundamental questions in the Gallup Q12, the Gallup Organization's seminal employee engagement survey, is, "Do you know what is expected of you at work?" It is shocking to recognize just how many people don't. Why? Because very few

employees have tangible, measurable key performance indicators (KPIs) or job objectives to strive for.

This lack of specific, measurable goals and objectives is also the primary cause of performance problems.

Why else are objectives important? Employees need to know what is expected of them and how success is measured. But more than that, people are naturally goal-oriented and need something concrete to strive for to feel a sense of certainty. Goals or objectives can also give them a sense of how they fit into the overall company direction.

Objectives give you a common language to use with your people. And the ability to describe clearly the gap between where they are and where they need to be presents an opportunity for you to manage their performance early, quickly and effectively.

C = Career Development

Many studies list career development among the top three factors that employees use to determine whether to stay with their current employer or look for another job. Yet many managers avoid this topic like the plague for one of three reasons:

© iStock/skodonnell

- They themselves don't understand how to manage their own careers.
- They are afraid that if they help their staff manage their career better they will surpass them on the corporate ladder.
- They are afraid to talk about career development because they don't feel they can meet the employee's expectations. (This is especially true in smaller companies or niche functions where there is not a lot of vertical career opportunity available.)

If you yourself manage your career well you'll never have to worry about being surpassed. And good managers are typically recognized for developing staff well. So proper career management for both you and your staff is truly in your best interest.

Helping your staff manage their careers makes good business sense, too. Helping them understand what opportunities exist within your company (something they may not recognize without your help) will deter them from looking elsewhere, saving you the time, expense and frustration of having to replace them.

But how do we address the third point, career development? If you work in a small company or department, there just may not be that many opportunities to move up the career ladder. As a result, many managers are afraid of highlighting these limited career opportunities. The assumption here is that all staff are interested in vertical career development. But that simply isn't true. Many people want to manage career around family or just want to do interesting work in a good company with people they like.

All of your staff, though, want to learn, grow and develop horizontally. Experience tells us that if you help them recognize horizontal opportunities and honestly address their career aspirations, they become very loyal and they actually look for reasons to stay instead of opportunities to leave.

U = Underlying Motivators

The Underlying Motivators Conversation is designed to find out what your staff needs to be motivated to "go the extra mile," and how they respond to different types of motivation and praise. Each person is different in this area. Some respond to public acknowledgment, while others shy away from it, preferring instead a quiet "Well done" or "Good job." Some respond to competition (with themselves or others), while others wither and die at the thought of it.

Understanding these concepts and determining what will work for each individual is one of the most frustrating things managers encounter. However, by learning some very basic truths about how your people are "wired" mentally and emotionally, you can unlock the secrets of keeping them happily motivated.

S = Strengths

According to the Gallup Organization, teams that focus on using their strengths are 12.5 percent more productive.[16] You can think of a "strength" as an innate ability or behavioral pattern that is neurologically hardwired into the brain between the ages of 3 and 15.[17] The context of the be-

havior will change over time, but the pattern remains the same. So those children who share their toys in the sandbox at the age of five may very well become 15-year-olds who volunteer their time in school to help tutor less academically-gifted students; and 20 years later they may become the 35-year-olds who are the most collaborative in the workplace.

But a strength is not *simply* what you're good at. As we will see in Chapter 8, it's also what makes you *feel good*. After all, do you want to be asked to do activities day in, day out that you're good at, but which you absolutely hate?

The Gallup Organization reports that employees who use their strengths every day are six times more likely to be engaged at work.[18] If you can help your staff identify those behaviors that come naturally to them and work more in those areas and less in those that don't, you'll find your staff become much less stressed, more engaged and, of course, more productive.

Let's Get Started...

Now that we've discovered what your staff truly want and need to be fully engaged and productive, and how those Currencies of Choice map onto our 5 *FOCUSed* Conversations, in the rest of the book we will explore exactly how (and how often) to have these conversations. Each chapter will drill deeply into one category of conversation. In its pages, you will learn:

- Why the conversation is important
- What the conversation consists of
- How to hold the conversation (including exercises and tools to use)
- Finally, a useful summary of first steps so you can start implementing the 5 *FOCUSed* Conversations immediately

The process of changing the way you communicate with your staff may appear daunting at first, but experience shows that by taking it step by step, you can make significant changes quickly. The result will be a lifetime of more engaged, happier and more productive staff, as well as more free time, less stress and higher job satisfaction for yourself and your team.

Notes

3 | How to Use the *FOCUSed* Conversation Framework

> *If communication is not your top priority, all of your other priorities are at risk.*
>
> • **Bob Aronson**, Communications Consultant

You're committed to having regular, frequent, structured, proactive conversations with your staff around the five areas that will truly motivate and engage them. Now what?

In order to use this framework effectively you should follow the *Six Steps to Success:*

1. Classify your team and prioritize your time

2. Schedule and conduct the first meeting with your staff

3. Prepare for each meeting

4. Conduct the meeting

5. Document the meeting

6. Monitor progress throughout the month

But first, a word about frequency.

Frequency

The first and most important hurdle you will need to overcome is finding time in your calendar (and theirs) for regular, structured communication sessions with each of your staff. Remember, this is an investment, and like all investments, it will only happen if you — and they — make it mandatory to put in the time and effort needed.

In a perfect world, you will be having these conversations with all of your direct reports. However, if you absolutely cannot find 45 minutes to an hour for everyone, use the 80/20 rule: spend 80 percent of your time working with those who are in your top 20 percent.

You read that right — the top 20 percent — not your problem children, where most managers traditionally spend most of their time. (More on this in a minute.)

How frequent is "frequent"? When presented with this opportunity, some of your staff will want to meet all of the time, while others will not want to meet at all. We will discuss how and why individuals feel the way they do (and how to manage each scenario) in Chapter 7, The Underlying Motivators Conversation.

On average, though, you want to meet with each member of your staff monthly. Don't worry — you won't be having all five of these conversations every month. The program provides for monthly conversations around Feedback and Objectives, and then including sessions on Career Development, Underlying Motivators and Strengths three to four times per year on a rotating basis. (To download a *FOCUSed* Conversations Planning calendar, go to http://igniteglobal.com/mrfmbook/.)

> ### Meeting Frequency
>
> - Frequent communication is essential to employee engagement and productivity.
> - Find time for regular, *structured communication* sessions with each of your staff.
> - Suggest at least monthly, structured sessions.
> - Regular monthly sessions should include the 5 **FOCUSed** Conversations.
>   - *Monthly:* Feedback and Objectives
>   - *Rotating, every few months:* Career Development, Underlying Motivators and Strengths

So, where do you begin? The first step in the Six Steps to Success is to classify your team and prioritize your time.

1. Classify Your Team and Prioritize Your Time

Employees typically come in three "flavors." On one end of the spectrum you have your *Critical People.* These can be obvious: they are the real superstars who consistently under-promise and over-deliver. But they can also be not so obvious: those quiet achievers or "Steady Eddies." They may never be superstars — in fact they may barely be above mediocre — but they are consistent and reliable.

Critical People also can be those staff members who hold important intellectual property or jobs no one else wants to do. They may have great customer relationships or know a lot about the organization itself. In any case, you don't want to lose them. Critical People of all three types usually constitute from 10 to 20 percent of your staff.

Then there are the 60 to 70 percent I call the *Fat Middle*. They're the ones who do what it takes to get the job done but they will rarely go the extra mile. They're reliable if uninspired. But the Fat Middle can be motivated through the 5 **FOCUSed** Conversations — and, as you'll see later, by the time you spend mentoring the Critical People on your staff.

At the other end of the spectrum you have the 10 to 20 percent who are the *Squeaky Wheels*. There are two types. First are high performers who are also high maintenance (we'll talk about those in Chapter 7, The Underlying Motivators Conversation). The second are those who "squeak" because they present either a performance or a behavior problem.

It's often said that "the squeaky wheel gets the grease," and perhaps that's a good thing in a mechanic's workshop. In a business environment, however, it's a recipe for poor management, high staff turnover and low productivity. Spending an overabundance of time with these Squeaky Wheels quickly can become problematic.

Unfortunately, this is what most managers do. They spend time with those who demand their time — the Squeaky Wheels — many times to the detriment of the team and to themselves.

Spending too much time with your problematic Squeaky Wheels sends the wrong message to staff. It rewards poor performance and behavior instead of good performance and behavior. Instead, you should prioritize your time so that you *spend 80 percent of it with your Critical People and 20 percent split between the Squeaky Wheels and Fat Middle.*

A Classify and Prioritize Case Study

Mike was the CFO of a large manufacturing company in New Zealand. He was a great CFO and he took this job because it suited his strengths perfectly. The company was looking for a very strategic Head of Finance who could work in partnership with the company's CEO to take market share in existing markets, enter new markets and diversify their product line.

Mike also owned an art gallery on the side and worked hard during business hours, but appreciated the flexibility his previous roles afforded him that allowed him to leave work every day between 5 and 6 p.m.

When Mike started his new job he quickly realized that there was a huge problem. The way the department was set up he had to spend all of his time working on the financials and looking at the past instead of working with the CEO to plan the future. He also found himself working 70 to 80 hours per week.

Mike knew this was unsustainable for several reasons. He was not using his talents and would eventually become disengaged and frustrated. He was also not doing what he was hired to do, which would become a source of irritation to the CEO. Finally, he was not able to devote the time and attention to his other business, which not only made him unhappy but also made his business partner and wife unhappy. Any way you looked at it, the most likely scenario was that Mike and the company would part ways. But he didn't want that to happen.

Mike quickly sized the situation up. He had too many direct reports — in fact, all of the staff reported directly to him. He had too many staff tasked with doing routine, clerical work (in a large part because some were not particularly suited to their roles and his predecessor had hired more of them to get the job done). His mid-level staff members were not being used effectively, nor had they been given the responsibility to assist in managing the clerical staff.

So, he reorganized the department and prioritized his time. He decided who his high-potential staff members were (his Critical People) and redesigned their job descriptions to allow them to take on the responsibility of generating the financial reports and working on budgets. Those became his direct reports. He then empowered his direct reports and made them responsible for managing and/or mentoring the other staff. He supported them in determining which of his Squeaky Wheels needed training (and provided that), which needed a bit of motivation (which he accomplished in various ways) and which needed to be moved on (only two to three in total).

Within six to eight months Mike was back working a 40-hour work week and spending his time working with the CEO on strategy — exactly what he was hired to do.

As an added benefit, employee retention went up as a result of the staff being deployed properly, working together much more effectively and enjoying their own jobs to a much greater extent.

At this point you might be asking yourself, "Why should I spend time with the people that can take care of themselves? These are the people that I rely on, that consistently deliver. They don't need my help."

But they do! There are at least three reasons to spend 80 percent of your time with your Critical People rather than the Squeaky Wheels or Fat Middle.

1. Allowing them to mentor with and learn from you will help them grow and develop in their own careers — and as we've already seen in Chapter 2, this is one of the Currencies of Choice that is far better at motivating and driving performance than money.

2. If you don't give them the time and attention they deserve (and may crave) they may not understand how important they actually are to you, which can lead to frustration, hurt feelings and even a sense that they aren't appreciated. The number of people who walk into recruiters' offices looking for a new role because they didn't feel appreciated by their boss is astonishing — and easily avoided.

3. The third reason was discovered by the Gallup Organization and written about in *Discover Your Sales Strengths* by Benson Smith and Tony Rutigliano. It shows that successful managers spend more than three-quarters of their time with their star performers and new recruits instead of their mediocre or poor team members.[19] As the saying goes, "A rising tide lifts all boats." If you give your attention to and empower those of your staff who really want to perform, they will help you manage the others.

A Critical People Case Study

Kathy, the recruiter, was surprised to see Janet — she only took the appointment because she was curious. She knew Janet's boss, Marie, socially, and she knew how highly Marie thought of Janet. So when Janet told Kathy how under-appreciated she was in the department, Kathy had to stop her. She didn't want to tell Janet that she knew Marie or that she knew how important Janet was to Marie and the team. But she encouraged her to sit down with Marie to talk about her position with the company. After much discussion, Janet finally agreed.

A week later, Janet told Kathy that she and Marie finally had the conversation that they should have had before Janet looked for another job. And boy, was she glad she did. Marie not only told Janet how highly she thought of her, she also discussed her future plans for both of them. It seems that Marie had her eye on another role within the company, and in Marie's mind, Janet was her most likely successor.

They also talked about Janet's workload and agreed that she was doing too much. Janet had taken on extra responsibilities to learn new skills, but she'd developed a habit of not being able to say no. As a result, Janet had become overworked and very stressed out. Marie agreed that Janet needed help and committed to hire another part-time person for the team.

Janet couldn't thank Kathy enough for encouraging her to have the conversation with Marie. Had she not done so, she may very well have left a job she loved — and missed out on a great opportunity for the future. And Marie would have lost her potential successor – without ever knowing why.

So what about your Squeaky Wheels? Should you just ignore them? Well, yes…maybe. Maybe some of your Squeaky Wheels squeak *just* to get your time and attention, like a child who is naughty simply because they crave love and attention from Mom and Dad. Some adults are not much different; so try ignoring your Squeaky Wheels and see if some stop squeaking naturally.

If ignoring them isn't the answer then there are three other possible scenarios.

Scenario #1: Use the Objectives Conversation, discussed in Chapter 5, to set more clear objectives or key performance indicators (KPIs), give them the necessary training they need to accomplish those and then hold them accountable for doing so.

Scenario #2: Use the other **FOCUSed** Conversations to uncover their personal Currencies of Choice and use those to motivate them to a higher level of performance or better behavior.

Scenario #3: Move them on. Let them squeak on someone else's bus.

Miraculously, when this 80/20 strategy is put into place, the Fat Middle takes care of itself. The good ones want to be part of the "cool kids club," and have the time and attention they see managers giving to the Critical People. They tend to become more engaged and to develop more quickly, especially if the manager empowers the Critical People to help train, mentor and motivate the Fat Middle.

So, as tempting as it feels to grease that Squeaky Wheel, you need to take a different approach. By spending *more* time with your Critical People, you will increase productivity, manage your time effectively, have more engaged staff and increase retention rates. Not only that, you will be spending more time working with those that want to be there, want to perform and behave well and want to help you meet your goals. Bottom line, *you* just might have more fun in your own job.

Again, if you absolutely don't have time to have thorough conversations with all of your staff members, be sure that you prioritize your Critical People. Schedule monthly conversations with them, put them in both sets of calendars and do not miss these meetings.

But if you do make the investment of your time with all of your staff, you will more than likely find within six to eight months that you have more time and that your team is more productive. Most managers never turn back once they make this discovery.

2. Schedule and Conduct the First Meeting with Your Staff

"Why are we meeting?"

Wait! Before you do step #2 you need to make sure that you answer the question that will be on everyone's minds: "Why are we meeting?"

People tend to go to the worst-case scenario first. So, it's very likely that when your staff gets wind of the fact that you want to meet with them monthly, their first question will be something like, "What's wrong? Is the company in trouble? Am I in trouble? What have I done wrong?"

Make sure that you alleviate these concerns by holding an impromptu meeting with your entire staff, together or separately, to discuss the purpose of these meetings and how they will benefit from them.

Begin by telling them that these monthly conversations are designed to help them be more successful in their roles and manage their careers so that they are able to achieve their professional and personal goals. Tell them that you will be discussing a number of topics several times over the course of the year. These topics include:

- Acknowledging and praising them for their good work
- Helping them understand what they need to do to be successful in their role and addressing any potential obstacles to that success early
- Inviting them to give you feedback on what's working and what's not in their jobs or the organization
- Giving them the opportunity to voice ideas that could help the entire team, office or company
- Finding out more about what motivates them
- Helping them to discover what they are really good at and love doing day to day, and then assisting them in spending more of

their time doing those activities and discovering ways to manage or mitigate any weaknesses they may have

- Helping them to better manage their careers so they achieve their goals

Then schedule meetings with each member of your staff individually — and *don't reschedule or cancel*. It's important to treat these meetings as you would appointments with clients, external stakeholders or your own manager.

The First Meeting

Start by reminding them of the reasons behind the monthly meetings. Give them an overview of what lies ahead. And then, focus exclusively on feedback.

There are three reasons for this. First, as we have already seen in the Introduction, being appreciated is one of your staff's Currencies of Choice. If they have done something to deserve praise, start with that, even if you've previously praised them for it. Be authentic. Give praise where praise is due — don't make it up.

Second, they may be skeptical. That's okay: trust will grow over time.

Third, they may have quite a bit to say to you. Sit back and listen. If they feel comfortable enough, they may bring up a list of issues that have been simmering for a while. If they bring something up that you can address immediately, do so. If they bring things up that you can address over time, commit to a time frame for more study or action, and then stick to that. And if they voice issues or concerns over which you don't have control or which you do not want to change, manage their expectations. Acknowledge their concerns and then tell them why you cannot or do not want to take their suggestions on board. Be specific and lay out the business reasons behind your decision or share the obstacles you face yourself if it's something beyond your control. They will respect you for it.

A Managing Expectations Case Study

David is the Group Risk Manager for a very large building supplies company with operations in the U.S., Europe, Australia and New Zealand. Throughout his career David has been able to develop enviable relationships with his staff. He has very, very low employee turnover and is highly respected and admired.

When asked his secret, David replies, "It's simple. When I first take over a team I meet with them individually and ask what their biggest obstacle to getting their job done might be. When they tell me (and they always do because it's typically been brewing for a long time), I make it a priority to fix it. Sometimes it's a simple matter that can be fixed straight away. Other times it takes a while. When it's a longer-term scenario I always keep them informed on the progress. I make sure that they never forget that I'm working on their behalf. I've only ever failed to fix something that was mentioned in these conversations once in my career. But the fact that I tried engendered more loyalty and trust that I could have ever imagined."

3. Prepare for Each Meeting

Proper preparation prevents poor performance. Not only does it prevent you from losing trust and respect from your staff by performing poorly in these meetings, it will also help manage their performance so you have fewer staff that perform poorly on the job. So pre-plan each conversation — don't let it devolve into an unstructured "catch up."

Remember, each month you will have the Feedback and Objectives Conversations. The other three conversations are to be included three to four times per year on a rolling basis.

There are several tools that can help you prepare for your monthly meetings with staff members. First, the *FOCUSed* Conversation Planner (available at http://igniteglobal.com/mrfmbook/) provides a framework for your monthly conversations. You can follow this calendar as a guide for at least the first few months until you become comfortable with this program, at which time you may find that you would like to modify it to suit your needs better. Please feel free to do so. The main point of this program is to have conversations about your staff members' Currencies of Choice on a regular basis.

Second, use the tips in each of the following chapters on the individual conversations to plan for specific meetings. Each chapter includes a list of *Conversation Starters.* These Conversation Starters are just that: starters designed to get the ball rolling. The ones that are included in this book are not meant to be exhaustive or definitive. Feel free to add or modify to suit your needs.

For easy reference, you can download the complete list of Conversation Starters for each of the 5 *FOCUSed* Conversations at http://igniteglobal.com/mrfmbook/.

4. Conduct the Meeting

The remainder of this book will cover this point in much more detail. Remember, each meeting includes the Feedback and Objectives Conversations. You may choose to begin with those, or to cover the other material first. Either way, make sure that you cover all planned topics within the time frame allowed, or schedule a follow-on meeting.

Best practice is to allocate time for each topic of conversation and then schedule a follow up if the entire conversation cannot be accomplished in the allocated time. This will help you manage your time as well as your staff's.

5. Document the Meeting

During or after the meeting, be sure to document any notes and fill out any required action items. You can also use the **FOCUSed** Conversation Planner for this purpose.

Although it should be obvious, there are two reasons to document the meetings:

1.   To remember what was discussed at prior meetings and keep track of any action items assigned to either you or your staff

2.   For performance management purposes — needed in the (hopefully decreasing) incidences of having to conduct remedial performance management

6. Monitor Progress throughout the Month

No one likes to be micro-managed, but be sure to check in on your team's progress throughout the month so you can identify and rectify any challenges that might occur. You will also want to assure staff members that if they need anything between scheduled sessions, you are here to help.

Remember, this is an investment. At first glance, this may feel like quite a bit of work, but once you become comfortable with this program your ability to manage becomes much easier and your staff members become much more engaged and productive. The end result will be a more engaged, more productive, highly performing team — which means less personal stress and more time for you to get on with your own work.

Putting It into Action:
First Steps from This Chapter

1. Classify your team. Who are your:
   a. Critical People
   b. Squeaky Wheels
   c. Fat Middle

2. Have an impromptu meeting with all of your staff (together or separately) to tell them about the monthly conversations and *why these meetings will benefit them.*

3. Schedule time in the calendars of you and each staff member for the first meeting.

———•———

The world's greatest achievers have been those who have always stayed focused on their goals and have been consistent in their efforts.

Roopleen
Words to Inspire the Winner in YOU

———•———

Notes

4 | *FOCUSed* Conversation #1:

The Feedback Conversation

© iStock/alephx1

The Feedback Conversation at a Glance

1. Share company news/updates.

2. Give praise where praise is due.

3. Give them a voice.

Why It's Important

Have you ever had a boss who gave you no feedback whatsoever? How did that make you feel?

Are you that boss?

The statistics on the importance of feedback are staggering. According to a 2009 Gallup Organization study of the impact of manager feedback on employee engagement:

- Employees receiving predominantly negative feedback from their manager are over 20 times *more likely to be engaged* than those receiving little or no feedback.
- Employees ignored by their manager are twice as likely to be *actively disengaged* compared with workers whose manager focuses on their weaknesses.
- Managers giving little or no feedback to employees results in 4 out of 10 workers being actively disengaged.
- Managers giving little or no feedback to their workers fail to engage 98 percent of them.[20]

This shows that even *negative* feedback is better than *no* feedback! But positive feedback reaps even more results. The same study shows that:

- Managers focusing on employee strengths are 30 times more likely to manage actively engaged workers, compared with managers denying feedback.
- Managers focusing on employee strengths are one-third more likely to manage actively engaged employees, compared with managers focusing on weaknesses.

We will talk more about these findings in Chapter 8, The Strengths Conversation. But consider these results as related to feedback specifically. They clearly say that *feedback of any sort is crucial to employee engagement, but positive feedback nets significantly greater results.*

But it's not just Gallup that reports staggering findings related to praise and productivity. A 2004 study by the University of Michigan reported that high-performing teams used about six times as many positive comments for every negative one. Conversely, it found that low-performing teams averaged three negative comments for every positive one.[21] And, according to a 2013 CNN article about feedback, "Denmark-based Alexander Kjerulf, who studies happiness at work, said his organization conducted a survey that found lack of praise and recognition to be the No. 2 factor making people unhappy at their jobs."[22]

This mirrors Ignite Global's own research. Remember the 5,000 exit interviews that led to the Currencies of Choice? One of these Currencies of Choice is that staff members want to be appreciated — not a surprise given the findings above.

That doesn't mean that you shouldn't give negative or constructive feedback. Indeed you should, and we will talk more about that in Chapter 5, The Objectives Conversation. It does mean that positive feedback is so important that it deserves its own conversation. This is why the Feedback Conversation is not meant to be a performance management conversation: it's neither the time nor place to discuss operational issues or give "constructive" feedback on performance. Again, this is reserved for the Objectives Conversation.

But more than that, from a neurological perspective positive feedback or praise is best separated from constructive feedback.

According to Sue Langley, founder and CEO of the Langley Group, a consulting firm specializing in emotional intelligence in the workplace, "Conventional wisdom suggests praising people and giving constructive feedback in the same conversation — a feedback sandwich, if you will. Unfortunately, this conventional wisdom can backfire on you. People are not stupid, if they suspect they are going to be given a negative message then starting with a positive will leave them wondering 'yeah, but....' They are waiting for the filling in the sandwich without really processing the positive. They can then start to raise their defenses, making the constructive feedback less potent as well.

"If you end on a positive you often leave the person feeling good, which is lovely, but you have probably detracted from the point of the feedback and the person walks away without actually taking in the constructive coaching you wanted to get across. So combining positive with negative, despite conventional wisdom, dilutes both messages."

———•———

Despite what conventional wisdom has taught us, the feedback sandwich (good–bad–good) doesn't work. It dilutes both messages and staff is left feeling confused.

Sue Langley

Founder and CEO, The Langley Group

———•———

The flip side of feedback, of course, is giving your staff a voice — another of our Currencies of Choice. Allowing them to give you open, honest feedback about what's working, what's not, and any ideas or suggestions they may have to help them do their job better or to help the team or the organization as a whole not only promotes better communication within the organization, it also gives staff a sense that they can control their own destiny and contribute to the organization from a wider perspective. As we will see in the chapter on the Underlying Motivators Conversation, these are two of the strongest intrinsic or internal drivers for staff and hold far more sway than external motivators such as pay and benefits.

Transparent communication is a hallmark of the Social Age organization. Think back to the Towers Watson statistic from Chapter 2 showing that companies with robust communication are 1.7 times more likely to outperform their peers. This communication must be two-way, though, which is why allowing staff to have a voice is so important.

It's also critical to the productivity of your workplace for you to disseminate relevant information to all layers of staff about what is going on within the organization. Doing so consistently, frequently and repetitively also prevents the grapevine from going into overdrive, which it does when staff are left to guess what is going on.

Your aim as a strong manager is to stop the grapevine in its tracks by always being clear with internal communication. Remember, people's perception about what is happening is typically far worse than the reality.

———•———

Transparent communication is key to creating a culture of innovation. It's important that people understand what each other are working on and how what they are working on aligns with company goals and values, and that they feel able to share knowledge and ideas and give constructive feedback to all levels of the organization openly and honestly.

Joris Juijke
VP Human Resources and Talent, Squarespace

———•———

Now that we understand why the Feedback Conversation is so important, let's talk about what it is and how to prepare for holding Feedback Conversations with your staff.

What is the Feedback Conversation?

Remember, the Feedback Conversation consists of three parts:

1. Sharing company news/updates
2. Giving praise where praise is due
3. Giving them a voice

Let's discuss the three parts of the Feedback Conversation in more depth.

1. Share Company News/Updates

As you will see throughout this book, the monthly conversations are just a piece of the puzzle (albeit a very important one) to creating a healthy work environment with engaged and productive staff. So let's take a step back and look at organizational updates from a broader perspective.

Best practice is to update staff in a variety of ways and in a regular manner. People learn and remember information differently. Some learn and remember better if they read it, others if they hear it and still others if they experience it. This means that effective communication needs to be both written and verbal. And for those experiential learners it's best if they can touch and feel it (difficult to do when simply relaying information, but a good practice to keep in mind while training staff).

Organizations with the most robust communication routinely (weekly, bi-weekly or monthly) relay information to staff through a combination of:

- Newsletters
- Emails with specific updates
- Policy updates
- Company website
- Company intranet
- Social media
- "Town Hall" meetings
- One-on-one meetings between managers and staff
- Video updates

Regardless of how you update staff be sure to include:

- Who we're hiring
- Who's leaving us and why
- Revenue, profitability or other financial results

- Team or company results or metrics (outside of revenue, profitability or other financial results)
- New initiatives
- New products, markets or geographies that we may be expanding into and why
- Products, markets or geographies that we are exiting and why
- Where we're going this month, quarter or year
- Our strategic plan and milestones to achieve that
- What the CEO is doing

Now let's look at how this relates to our monthly conversations. As you can see above, updating staff on what is happening in the organization is more involved than sitting down one-on-one with staff.

You don't want to use the monthly conversations as the exclusive mechanism to deliver company updates. During these conversations you want to do two things:

1. Talk to them one-on-one about any sensitive topics that are not for wide distribution, directly affect them or that you suspect to which they may react negatively.
2. Remind them about any updates that have occurred within the last month and ask if they have any questions about them.

The first point should be obvious. You want to deliver any potential negative news or sensitive information in person.

The second point is important from two perspectives. First of all, in this digital age we are bombarded with information. Not everyone will be aware of the updates that are disseminated widely because they may not have opened that email, read that intranet post, clicked on the link or been at the Town Hall meeting with the CEO. And even if they have read it, they may not remember it because it's not "top of mind" with everything else they have on their plate.

The real point here is that you don't have to rehash the information. The monthly meeting is simply your opportunity to point them to the specific place where they can find it.

Asking if they have any questions or discussing the information also gives you the opportunity to clear up any misconceptions or misunderstandings. And it's a great way of circumventing the inevitable, "But I didn't know about that!" comment.

So, aim to keep this part of the conversation short, sharp, real and to the point. Remember, your intention is to keep your staff informed, give them feedback overall on how the organization is going and stop the grapevine in its tracks.

And don't forget, these days the grapevine includes texting, emails, Skype, YouTube, Instagram, Glassdoor and Facebook — just to name a few of the many methods of sharing misinformation. Give your staff information they want to share with their friends and families — if you keep them informed you will watch their engagement levels grow.

2. Give Praise Where Praise is Due

This should be self-explanatory. Catch them doing things right, and don't wait to praise them until your monthly conversation: praise in real time. But beware, as we will discover in the chapter on the Underlying Motivators Conversation, the old adage of "Praise in public, correct in private" may not apply to everyone (at least for praise).

All this conversation is meant to do is to provide a trigger for you to think about what they have done in the last month that is praiseworthy and to ask yourself if you've previously praised them for it. If not, be sure to do so. Even if you have, it might be worthwhile to mention it again. Remember the 6:1 ratio above?

How to Give Praise

It's important that your praise is authentic. If they truly have not done any-thing that is worthy of praise, don't praise them. But when you do, make sure it's more than just a "Great job." Praise, like constructive feedback, is much more impactful if it's specific.

So, instead of saying something like, "Great job in the meeting last week," talk specifically about what impressed you. You might want to phrase it like this:

> "I really want to tell you again how impressed I was
> with your participation in the marketing meeting last
> Thursday. You weren't afraid to voice your opinion
> and your argument was well thought out, articulate
> and compelling. Even though they didn't accept your
> suggestion, you should be proud of your contribution."

Other Conversation Starters for praising a staff member include:

- *I just wanted to say well done on....*
- *I really appreciated....*

(For a full list of Conversation Starters go to http://igniteglobal.com/mrfmbook/.)

A Praise Case Study

A mid-sized financial services firm undertook an employee engagement survey in 2010. It didn't go well: they scored somewhere in the mid-60's, showing a workforce that was passively engaged at best. Several recommendations came out of this survey, but due to market and organizational factors (including a very difficult merger) only one was implemented: praise.

They trained their managers on the importance of praise and on how to deliver it effectively. They made it a part of their organizational culture. And that's all they did.

When they undertook their next Employee Engagement Survey in 2012 they didn't expect much of an increase. But to the surprise (and delight) of the CEO and the Board, their engagement numbers skyrocketed to an astonishing 91 percent!

3. Give Them a Voice

Finally, allow your staff members to voice their opinions, objections, suggestions and ideas. Allow them to give you feedback. What's working for them? What do they like about the organization, the team, your management style?

What's not working? What obstacles are preventing them from doing their best work? What else do they need to be successful?

What ideas do they have to improve productivity, efficiency, customer service? Do they have ideas for new products, lines of business or anything else to help grow the company? Many innovations come from the grass roots. Sure, some come from steering committees, project teams, marketing departments and the like. But many others come from people like John Doe in Accounting, who had a great idea in the shower. Allow those shower ideas to come out — who knows, one of them may just turn into the next big step for your organization.

Yes, you as a manager may need to have a bit of a thick skin to hear some of what your staff says, but if you can truly allow open, honest feedback both you and they will grow.

How to Let Them Have a Voice

Some staff won't be shy in giving you open, honest feedback. For those, just asking a few questions will get the ball rolling.

Generational Differences

Gen Y's, Millennials, whatever you might call them: those born after 1980 are typically not shy in coming forward to voice their ideas and opinions. For this generation, the key might be to manage their expectations.

Research indicates that they want to be trained and mentored. They actually want structure. So don't be afraid to tell them that their ideas won't work, but tell them why they won't work, using facts, figures, reasoning and sound analysis. Don't just tell them, "We tried that before and it didn't work." They will have no patience for this rhetoric.

On the other hand, the oldest generation in the workforce, the Baby Boomers (born between 1946 and 1964), were raised to be "seen and not heard." This generation (along with members of Gen X, to some extent) need to be encouraged to speak up. Make it safe for them to voice their opinions.

Who knows? Your staff, regardless of their generation, may have the next great idea!

Others won't feel comfortable at all being honest. If this is the case, you might need to start slow. Encourage their feedback by asking great questions (you can find examples below) and then build trusting by acting on what they say. Take any constructive criticism positively and, if you truly believe they have a point, make a commitment to address it. Implement any suggestions you can, but if you can't, go back to them later and tell them that you've considered their suggestion and appreciate it, but can't implement it. Then give them *specific reasons* why it can't be implemented and encourage them to keep the suggestions coming.

Here are some Conversation Starters you can use to open up this part of the conversation.

Conversation Starters

- *What is your biggest frustration or roadblock in doing your best work? How would you suggest solving this issue?*
- *What do you like the best about your job these days?*
- *I'd like to talk about.... How did you think it went? What frustrated you or gave you the biggest problems?*
- *How do you think...could be done better?*
- *What suggestions do you have in the area of...?*
- *Tell me what worked during the...*
- *Tell me what didn't work on...*
- *How would you suggest we do...next time?*

How to Devise Your Own Questions

Reflect on what things have been happening within the organization recently and consider building questions around specific incidents. For example, say you were seeking feedback on a corporate conference the staff member recently attended. Some of the questions you could ask include:

- *With our conference last month, I would really appreciate some constructive feedback from you. What were the highlights for you?*
- *What could we have done better?*
- *What were the best parts of the conference?*
- *What were the duds or parts that just didn't work?*
- *What were the general feelings from the staff about the events?*
- *Do you have any suggestions for how we could improve the event next year?*
- *If we didn't hold a conference next year, what would you suggest we replace it with?*

A Word of Warning

Don't let these conversations turn into complaint sessions. At first, if the staff member has pent-up frustrations or a lot to say, you might need to just let them vent. That's okay. Everyone needs to blow off steam once in awhile. Better they blow off steam with you than on Facebook, Twitter or Glassdoor. But if this becomes a pattern nip it in the bud — quickly. Train them to bring solutions to the table as well as problems.

How to Prepare for the Feedback Conversation

The Feedback Conversation is actually the easiest conversation to have. To prepare, ask yourself three questions.

1. What organizational updates have occurred within the last month?

    a. Are there any that directly affect them about which I need to speak with them in depth?

    b. Are there any to which they may have had a negative reaction?

    c. Where can I point them to if they are unaware or don't remember this news?

2. What have they done that is worthy of praise?

    a. Have I previously praised them for it? If not, make it a point to do so (more on this below). If so, does it bear repeating?

3. Do I think they have something to say to me? If so, make it a point to ask them about it specifically.

Conclusion

While the Feedback Conversation is the typically the easiest conversation to prepare for and conduct, in many ways it is also the most important. As we've seen in the statistics above, both open, honest communication as well as positive feedback make a significant difference to employee engagement and effectiveness. Make sure to treat it with the importance it deserves.

Utilize all three aspects of the Feedback Conversation every month. The outcome will be increased trust and respect — which is, not at all coincidentally, the first Currency of Choice.

Putting It into Action:
First Steps from This Chapter

It's time for your first meeting with your staff.

1. What do you need to share with them about the organization? What updates have occurred within the last month? Do any of these updates affect them directly? What sources of information do you need to offer them if they're unaware or don't remember the news?

2. What have they done that's worthy of praise? Even if you've praised them for this before, use this as an opportunity to practice phrasing the praise in specific terms and start the conversation with that.

3. Do you think they have something to say to you? If so, structure questions designed to elicit feedback from them on whatever that might be. If not, choose several of the Conversation Starters (or design your own) to ask them for feedback. Remember, some of your staff will be very open with you immediately, with others it may take some time.

4. Sit back and listen. Let them vent in the first meeting. Sometimes it may take awhile for them to get everything they have to say off of their chest.

5. Regardless of whether they have a little or a lot to say, end the meeting with specific action items. Commit to whatever falls under your responsibility *and keep your commitments.* Get them to commit to theirs with milestones, timelines and deliverables.

6. Document the conversation (or have them do this) and agree via email.

The people who get on in this world are people who get up and look for the circumstances they want, and, if they can't find them, make them.

George Bernard Shaw

5 | *FOCUSed* Conversation #2:

The Objectives Conversation

Evaluation

☐ OUTSTANDING
☐ Excellent
☐ Very Good
☐ Average
☐ Below Average

© Shutterstock/Michael D Brown

The Objectives Conversation at a Glance

1. Set specific, measurable job objectives and agree on them with each staff member.

   • Eliminate as much grey area as you can.

2. Review objectives quarterly and adjust for circumstantial changes.

3. Check in monthly for accountability.

   • Are they on track to meet their goals/achieve their objectives?

   • If not, why not? Do they need more time, training, resources?

   • What other obstacles are in their way?

4. Manage the gap and course correct.

Why It's Important

No one starts a job saying, "I really want to suck at this!" Or if they do, you've clearly hired the wrong person — but that's for another book in this series.

Most people are wired to want to succeed. As we saw in Chapter 2, one of your staff's Currencies of Choice is, "Understand how to be successful in their role."

In order to do that, they need to understand what they are responsible for accomplishing. Not doing — accomplishing. And how that will be measured.

Similarly, many (if not most) performance management problems could be avoided with more clearly defined and better articulated job objectives. The way most job objectives are written, there is too much room for interpretation.

Clearly stated job objectives are fundamental for employee performance. Much like a road map, they give the employee a clear direction in which to go and they give the manager a clear sense of whether the employee is going to reach their destination. If not, they should also give a clear picture of why the staff member is on the wrong track.

© iStock/binabina

An Objectives Case Study

Leigh had the potential to be an excellent salesperson. Her manager thought so. In fact, everyone in the company agreed. Why then was Leigh failing — to the point that her previous manager had put her on a 90-day probationary plan prior to leaving recently for his new role within the company?

Leigh's new manager, Kate, was at her wit's end. She'd talked to Leigh extensively and she knew that Leigh was having the right conversations with her prospects, but she hadn't been able to get enough of them "over the line" to make her sales targets.

Leigh knew what her sales targets were — in fact, she had quoted them many times during the last month to Kate. She knew how these were being measured and which report to pull from the system to get her up-to-date figures. But every time she (and Kate) looked at this report they both saw the glaringly obvious: Leigh was failing.

Kate decided to have one last conversation with Leigh before her probation was up to see if she could turn the situation around. They started to drill more deeply into creating a pipeline. To her astonishment, Leigh had never been given the company metrics on how many calls and visits it typically takes to close a deal!

Kate decided to refocus Leigh on objectives that she could more easily accomplish. Instead of looking at weekly sales figures, they started to focus on daily calls and weekly client visits. These were metrics that Leigh could get excited about! They were tangible and she felt as though she had much more control in achieving them.

Kate also helped Leigh to discover that she needed assistance with planning her day. She was new to sales and didn't fully appreciate that there were times throughout the day when her prospects might be at their desks and more likely to answer the phone. Leigh was actually scheduling administrative tasks during peak calling times!

Kate then provided additional training to Leigh to instill some peak productivity habits (like clustering similar activities together and working in short, concentrated bursts followed by a mini break).

The efforts paid off — extraordinarily so. Kate won an award that year for being one of the top 10 offices in the region, despite the fact that when she took the office over in August of that year they were significantly behind budget. The improvement in a large part was due to Leigh's turnaround and contribution to office revenue.

And Leigh? She went on to become a top salesperson within the company for several years running. She received multiple promotions over the next 10 years, at which time she finally left — to start her own very successful business.

Let's look at a very simple example of the problem with most job objectives. If you were to pick up a job description written for a receptionist you might very likely see an objective like, "Answer phones and greet customers."

At first look, that seems like a fine job objective. After all, that's what receptionists do, right?

Now let's imagine that we hire a receptionist who lets the phone ring 10 to 12 times on average before picking it up. Or that they let customers who appear at the front desk stand there for several minutes before even acknowledging them. And when they do, finally acknowledge them it's with a curt, "Yes?"

Is that acceptable behavior in your eyes? Would you be happy with their performance? Probably not.

But with a job objective written this ambiguously, do you have any recourse if you try to point this out as being unacceptable? No, you don't.

According to the Wynhurst Group (a consulting group specializing in HR strategy and employee development), 22 percent of employee turnover occurs within the first 45 days of employment.[23] Quite possibly, this is partially due to new staff not clearly understanding what they are responsible for doing. Conversely, the manager may have failed to thoroughly define in his or her own mind the actual requirements of the role prior to hiring.

> Most performance issues stem from a disconnect between what the manager perceives as meeting objectives and what the staff member perceives as meeting them.
>
> *To drastically reduce performance issues managers must clearly define and articulate expectations.*
>
> *Yet few do.*

In any case, as time goes on, if the manager fails to check in with staff members, actual performance may stray further and further from their desired performance until one day the manager realizes that the staff member has a performance problem. Unfortunately, by this time it may be too late to do anything about it. The manager is frustrated with the staff member: if someone has the abilities, skills and experience to do the job, why isn't he or she doing it better? At the same time, the employee may feel as though he or she has been set up to fail.

And this doesn't happen with just clerical positions or inexperienced staff. Versions of this scenario occur at the highest level. What about a CEO who has been tasked, "To drive profitability and growth"? If the company is in a restricted geography, a mature market or an overly regulated environment, the CEO may be thrilled with a 3 percent increase year on year. But if the Board is expecting 10 percent, the CEO could be fired.

Now, you might be saying to yourself, "They should have talked about this up front and agreed to the projections." And you would be right — but just because they should have does not mean they did. These scenarios happen all of the time.

Let's look at an example that might hit closer to home. Do you have an objective in your job description that says something like, "Responsible for coaching and managing staff"? That's terrific! But what does that actually mean? Are you measured on your employee retention rate? What about your ability to grow staff? Or your team's cumulative performance review scores? Do you even know what the measurements are for this objective?

Under our current, antiquated, yearly performance management paradigm, many staff (including managers because they are employees too) don't actually find out they are failing in their manager's eyes until that review. Not only is this unfair — it's unproductive.

———•———

(Performance appraisals) are an artifact from traditional top-down organizations where we had to "weed out" the bottom performers every year. By forcing managers to rate people once per year we can have annual talent reviews and decide who gets more money, who to promote, and who to let go.

Josh Bersin, "Time to Scrap Performance Appraisals?"

———•———

However, there's another way to manage, measure and evaluate performance, and that's with the 5 **FOCUSed** Conversations — and the Objectives Conversation in particular.

What Is the Objectives Conversation?

In order not only to help your staff understand what they need to do to be successful in their role but also to more efficiently and effectively manage their performance, you need to set clear and specific, measurable job objectives and then regularly check in with your people to review their progress in achieving those objectives, providing any additional training or resources needed along the way and course correcting early for any identified gaps between your expectation and theirs. That is what the Objectives Conversation is all about.

Let's look more closely at what this means.

What are Job Objectives?

Objectives (1) are outcomes, not tasks and (2) can typically be measured.

As we will see in Chapter 7, The Underlying Motivators Conversation, everyone wants to feel as though they are in control of their own destiny. Applied to this conversation, that means that staff wants to be given clear guidelines on *what* to accomplish and left to work out for themselves *how* to accomplish it, using their unique skills, abilities and talents.

Job objectives fulfill three purposes:

1. They help define what is required in a role. This makes it much easier to identify the type of person needed for an open job.

2. They form the basis of a well-structured probationary period framework. This is essential to ensure that any bad hires are dealt with immediately and do not cause performance and/or behavioral problems.

3. They form the foundation of an effective performance management system, whether a formal performance review or simply keeping performance on track to meet goals.

There are actually two major problems with most job objectives. The first is that, instead of defining the *what,* many describe the *how.* The second, as we've already seen, is that they do not describe how success will be measured.

Let's look back at the objective for our receptionist example, because this example illustrates both problems. The objective to "answer phones and greet customers" might look like a *what,* but is actually a *how.* A better *what* might read something like:

> *As the first point of contact with ABC Company, this position is responsible for greeting everyone, by phone or in person, quickly and professionally and by providing assistance to help them with their specific inquiry or need. To accomplish this you must:*
>
> - *Answer all phone calls within an average of three rings*
> - *Greet (or acknowledge if otherwise engaged) customers at the front desk within a minute of arrival*

Written in this manner, this objective also provides the criteria by which success is measured. They either answer the phone within three rings or they don't. They either greet customers within one minute or they don't.

Of course, they will need to be trained on the appropriate greeting, how to route the actual phone calls, who to screen for and who to pass through, etc. But these are training issues to refine the *how.*

You may also want to add other measurable criteria to this as well. For instance, if you regularly survey customers on their experience you might want to add something like, "A result of 85 percent is expected to be maintained on question 11 of the quarterly Customer Satisfaction Survey, 'Do you find our Receptionist professional and helpful?' "

The added benefit of stating this objective like this, "As the first point of contact with ABC Company, this position is responsible for greeting everyone, by phone or in person, quickly and professionally and by providing assistance to help them with their specific inquiry or need," is that it gives them a sense of how they fit into the organization and what their purpose is. As we will see in the chapter on the Underlying Motivators Conversation, a sense of community or purpose is also paramount to an employee's well-being.

If job objectives are tied to company mission, vision and values, they also can give your employees a sense of how they fit into the overall company.

Now let's look at how we might rewrite the other two examples above so that they are stated in terms of deliverables or outcomes and the criteria by which the staff member will be measured is made clear.

The original CEO objective, "To drive profitability and growth," might be re-written as, "To grow the company in line with our five-year Strategic Plan and to meet shareholder expectations, you are responsible for increasing year-on-year profitability by at least 5 percent for the next three years through a combination of enhanced revenue and cost control measures. Specific revenue targets to accomplish this goal are outlined in the Strategic Plan by geography, and cost control measures shall not result in a reduction of headcount."

Again, this gives the CEO a sense of how they fit into the overall picture and, while it gives parameters, it does not tell the CEO *how* to do the job. But it does give a very clear indication of criteria by which success will be measured. Note, though, that it refers the CEO to another document, the Strategic Plan. You don't have to reinvent the wheel when writing great job objectives. If something is spelled out elsewhere, simply refer to that.

Job objectives typically fall into four categories:

1. **Financial:** Directly impacts the bottom line either through revenue enhancement or cost savings

2. **People:** Includes KPIs regarding their direct reports, their team or potentially even their own manager

3. **Customer/Stakeholder:** KPIs regarding internal or external customers or stakeholders

4. **Process:** Tasks they need to do to complete their job (i.e. filling in time sheets or completing business plans)

How to Write a Job Objective

Now, let's practice writing a job objective in this way. And, what better way to start than by rewriting your own objective of, "Responsible for coaching and managing staff"?

To write a robust job objective you want to ask yourself three questions:

1. What is the outcome to be achieved?
2. How will it be measured?
3. Does this align with a larger purpose or integrate into a community?

What outcome would you want to achieve by coaching and managing staff? Here are some thoughts:

- To develop a talent pipeline for succession planning
- To reduce employee turnover
- To increase or maintain employee engagement
- To train staff to take positions within other areas of the company
- To maintain a competitive edge through innovative ideas or solutions

As you can see, the *what* then informs the measurement. Let's look at potential measures for each of these in turn.

- **To develop a talent pipeline for succession planning**
  - Two clear successors shall be identified by (date) as potential successors to (list positions) by meeting the criteria outlined in…
  - To successfully promote one staff member to (list position/s) within (timeframe)

- **To reduce employee turnover**
  - Employee turnover shall be maintained at (number) percent or less per annum
  - Employee retention shall increase by (number) percent per year over the next (number) years

- **To increase or maintain employee engagement**
  - Employee engagement scores shall be maintained at/increase by/to (number) percent by (date)

- **To train staff to take positions within other areas of the company**
  - (Number) percent of staff within your department will be selected for internal rotations each year

- **To maintain a competitive edge through innovative ideas or solutions**

  - This, of course, is a bit more subjective. You might look at attaching goals around industry rewards, new products launched or new business won, or this might need to stay as an aspirational goal, that is, one that cannot easily be measured.

The bottom line is that you want to measure what you can and be as specific as possible.

We've all learned about the *S.M.A.R.T. Goal* acronym, which stands for Specific, Measurable, Achievable, Relevant and Time-Bound. Don't worry if you can't remember them all. Just concentrate on your objectives being Specific and Measurable.

SMART Goals

GOAL SETTING	
Specific	Have you specified exactly *what*, *when, where* and *with whom?*
Measurable	What part of the goal can you measure? The number of forms processed, percentage of satisfied customers, increase in the number of enquiries?
Achievable	Feasible goals are more motivating than goals that are too difficult or overwhelming, considering the person's capabilities and the situation.
Relevant	Is the goal in line wiith the team's goals? Does it contribute to the organization's priorities or is it a nice "to do"?
Time-bound	Negotiate when each aspect of the goal will realistically be achieved.

The last question, of course, is, how does coaching and managing staff fit into overall company goals or help whomever is doing this job to feel like part of a larger community?

Here are some possibilities:

- To achieve (or maintain) company status as an "Employer of Choice"
- To achieve (or maintain) top worldwide ranking in (survey or results)
- To help maintain our enviable employer brand

- To establish (or maintain) our reputation as the "go-to" employer for all (list positions)

Let's play around with some of these combinations and embellish them with additional detail.

- In order to maintain our enviable position as Employer of Choice on the *XYZ List,* you will be responsible for helping to maintain our annual employee engagement score of X percent or above. Specifically, your department needs to maintain X percent as measured on the XYZ Survey. (*Note:* Coaching and managing staff — the original objective — is not even mentioned here.)

- Our employee turnover rate of 22 percent per year has been unacceptably high over the last three years. All managers will be responsible for coaching and managing staff more effectively in order to reduce unwanted turnover by three percentage points per year over the next two years.

- We are proud of the enviable reputation ABC Company has built when attracting talent. We are considered the "go-to" engineering consulting firm in our region. We believe this is, in part, due to the strong relationship between managers and staff. As X Manager, one of your responsibilities is to maintain that strong relationship through robust communication, coaching, training and mentoring. It is expected that doing this will result in at least one referral of a new staff member per year to the organization.

Okay... now it's your turn! Exercise: Write a Job Objective

Holding Your Staff Accountable for Achieving Job Objectives

This can only be done within the context of the conversation itself. This is true whether or not you follow this program. The difference is that if you do follow the program and have monthly *proactive* conversations with your staff, you will be able to "kill the monster while it's small" and avoid many major performance problems by making tiny course corrections along the way.

One of the most important benefits of clearly defined job objectives is that they give you a common language to use with your staff. And the gap between where they are and where they need to be presents an opportunity to talk about obstacles to remove or deficiencies in their performance.

Let's now turn to the actual Objectives Conversation.

How to Prepare

We've already talked about crafting robust job objectives, but how do you prepare for the actual conversation? That to a large extent depends on the level of your staff member. If you are working with a junior staff member you will want to be very directive in setting their objectives for them. The more senior the employee, or the more specialized their knowledge, the more collaborative you can (and should) be when setting objectives. The most senior members of staff (including managers and executives) could (and potentially should) set their own objective and then review them with you. The bottom line is that, regardless of the level of staff you're working with at the time, both you and they need to understand and agree that they are achievable.

Okay, so you've set and agreed on the job objectives with your staff. Great, that job's done.

Or is it?

As we've already established, we live and work in a very dynamic and changeable world these days. This means that what your staff is responsible for accomplishing can change very rapidly as well. Internal changes in direction or external factors relating to the economy, public policy, the regulatory environment or a number of other things may impact their ability to accomplish their goals — as can changes in the team such as hiring or losing someone, team dynamics or changes with other stakeholders within the organization.

———•———

Companies that set performance goals quarterly generate 31 percent greater returns from their performance process than those who do it annually, and those who do it monthly get even better results.
Josh Bersin, "Time to Scrap Performance Appraisals?"

———•———

As a result, you need to review these objectives quarterly. Most of the time if anything changes it will be minor; but several minor changes over time can add up to a major change. Lack of review and communication around these changes can result in significant gaps between what the manager expects and what the employee does.

So, set up a calendar reminder (or use the ***FOCUSed*** Conversation Planner available at http://igniteglobal.com/mrfmbook/) to review your objectives and consult with your staff quarterly.

But over and above this process, you must check in with them monthly for accountability. To prepare for these conversations, ask yourself:

1. **Do you know if they are achieving their goals?**
   - **If yes:** Acknowledge them (Feedback Conversation)
   - **If no:** Plan a discussion around why they are not achieving their goals and what you can do to help them.
     - Do they need more training?
     - Time?
     - Resources?
     - Access to stakeholders?

   Note: if this is a repetitive conversation you may need to move to a performance management program.

2. **Are there any behavioral problems to address? If so, plan for that conversation.**
   - **If you don't know:** Ask them to look at their job objectives prior to the meeting and be prepared to talk about whether or not they are on track to complete the objectives within the time frames specified. Let them know that if they aren't on track, you'd like to know as soon as possible so that you can give them the additional support (i.e. additional resources or

training, mentoring or guidance) they might need to successfully complete them.

- Make sure they realize this isn't a "witch hunt." You're not
out to rake them over the coals for not completing them.

How to Hold an Objective Setting or Review Conversation

By this point you already will have set objectives for a junior staff member,
or have planned how to set them for a more senior one. It's time to have the
actual conversation. You can open up the dialogue with these Conversation
Starters.

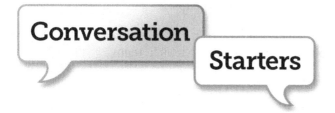

Conversation Starters to Set Job Objectives

- *I'd like to talk today about your job objectives. It's important that
you and I both understand what your responsibilities are so that
you know what you need to do to be successful and I have a way
to determine what additional support you might need. In order to
do that, I'd like to talk about what you're responsible for achieving
in this role and how we can formalize that into several specific job
objectives. After this conversation I'd like you to...*

- *I've written a few job objectives for you and I'd like to review them
with you now to make sure you understand what's expected and to
give you an opportunity to let me know what additional support
you might need to successfully complete them.*

- *Having reviewed the job objectives that I wrote for you, which do you think will come easily to you and which do you think you might need additional support with (i.e. additional resources or training, mentoring or guidance)?*

- *What is the purpose of your role, as you see it?*

- *Where do you fit into the team/organization?*

- *How do you feel that what you do impacts the overall goals of the team or organization?*

Note: You never want to say, "Please review these job objectives and let me know if you have any questions about them." They probably won't, but that doesn't mean they understand them. You want to engage them in a dialogue about the objectives so that you *know* beyond a shadow of a doubt that you and they are on the same page and that they understand what they are responsible for and how it will be measured.

Conversation Starters to Review Job Objectives

- *Let's look at your current job objectives. Do you think there might be anything that needs to be changed or modified? If so, why?*

- *I know that (fill in the blank) has changed since we last reviewed your objectives. How do you think this might impact them?*

How to Hold the Accountability Conversation

Optimally your staff members will have looked at their job objectives prior to the meeting and made note of whether they have successfully completed them or not, and if not, why not. The purpose of this conversation is to discover what additional support (i.e. additional resources or training, mentoring or guidance) they might need to successfully complete them — *not* to chastise them for not completing them or for getting off track.

Obviously, if this becomes a pattern or an issue you will want to go into performance management mode. This is outside the scope of this book because we truly believe that if you have these conversations regularly the need for such conversations will be drastically reduced.

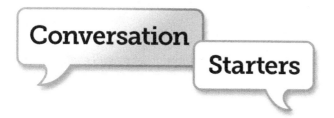

Conversation Starters for Accountability

Here are some Conversation Starters to help monitor progress and to hold them accountable for achieving their objectives.

- *Which objectives have you successfully completed, or are on track to complete? Is there anything I need to know or be aware of? If not complete, by when are they expected to be complete?*

- *Which objectives are you struggling with/having problems in achieving? What are the reasons that they are not going according to plan? What do you need to ensure they get back on track?*

One of the main misconceptions that you will have to overcome with this conversation is that you are micro-managing. That perception is a throwback to the old performance management framework. In order to break through this paradigm and move into a Social Age workplace you must (sometimes repeatedly) assure your staff that you are there to help. You believe you hired the right people and you want to give them the autonomy they need to accomplish what they were hired to do. But to do that, you need to make sure that you have regular conversations about what they might need to be successful.

If you genuinely come at this conversation from a place of support, the message will get through. It may take a while, but eventually it will happen, and then you can sit back and enjoy the results of greater productivity, innovation and a happier, more engaged staff.

Putting It into Action: First Steps from This Chapter

You've had your first, introductory meeting with your staff and covered the Feedback Conversation. It's now officially time to launch the monthly conversations, beginning with the Objectives Conversation. Begin with Month 1 if you're using the *FOCUSed* Conversation Planner.

1. Set objectives for any new staff or those whom do not have current objectives written.

2. Review the objectives for any staff that have them currently.
   - Are they written well using the guidelines from this chapter?
   - Are they still applicable and achievable given current circumstances?

   If either of the above are not the case, re-write them (either alone or in consultation with the staff member as applicable).

3. Have the conversation using the guidelines above.

4. Identify any gaps between your expectations and theirs. Is this a communication issue? A resource or support issue? A performance issue?

5. Determine an action plan (either alone or in consultation with your staff, your manager or your HR department) to bridge these gaps and document the conversation.

6. Ensure that your staff is aware of the action plan.

Notes

6 | *FOCUSed* Conversation #3:

The Career Development Conversation

© iStock/skodonnell

The Career Development Conversation at a Glance

1. Ensure your staff's professional goals are aligned with and support their personal ones.

   - Make sure that their professional goals are truly their own and that they are positively motivated about achieving them for the right reasons.

2. Determine what if anything about their job, their manager (you), their team or their work environment is frustrating them and how these frustrations can be fixed.

3. Help them build resilience to overcome setbacks.

Why It's Important

Why should you help your employees manage their careers better? Because it is one of the most effective and least costly employee engagement and retention strategies a company can offer.

Many studies list career development within the top three factors that employees gauge to determine whether to stay with their current employer or look for another. In fact, a 2013 survey by employment website Career-Builder found that workers who said they were likely to leave their jobs in the next year cited dissatisfaction with advancement opportunities at their current companies as the third most significant reason for leaving (behind concerns over salary and not feeling valued).[24]

But we've already seen this, right? Think back to the Currencies of Choice. Many of the 5,000 candidates interviewed in the process of developing those Currencies cited "career development" as the reason they were looking for another job.

But it's not just their ability to "climb the corporate ladder" that employees look for. Many of your staff desire a vertical career trajectory, to be sure — and many others simply want to manage career around family or to do interesting work for a company they can support. But the point is, *all* staff want to feel as though they are learning, growing and developing in their role, even if only a little. And if they don't feel that way, they have a tendency to "throw the baby out with the bathwater."

The problem is, many employees don't stop to think about or ask themselves why they have become frustrated or disenchanted in their jobs. They simply begin to recognize (either suddenly or over time) that they are unhappy. And if they become unhappy enough, or if the right person happens to catch them at the right time with another opportunity that sounds like it's the right one, they will leave.

Many, many, many employees who leave can and should be saved.
And you can save them very, very easily.

This is the *main* reason you should help your employees better manage their careers — because most of them do a terrible job of it themselves.

Multiple surveys indicate that career development ranks within the top three factors that employees evaluate when deciding whether to stay with or leave their current employer.

Most People Simply Go through Doors That Are Opened to Them

Of the 5,000 people that I interviewed during my 15-year career in recruiting, only 5 to 10 percent of them truly, *proactively* managed their careers. That is, they had a clear sense of where they wanted to go, why they wanted to go there and how they were going to get there.

© iStock/zentilia

Most people simply don't proactively manage their careers — and honestly, why would they? It's not something we are taught to do. Most people simply go through doors that are opened to them. You need a job (either because you become unhappy or circumstances change), so you go find a job. You need another job — you find another job.

If you're good at what you do (or sometimes just lucky) jobs will come to you. And this feels good! It's recognition for a job well done or it gives you a sense of acceptance and belonging. Many people take on new roles for this reason and this reason alone. They think to themselves, *They want me and think I can do the job, therefore it must be right for me!* Tragically, many times it's not.

A lot of people get lucky. They fall into the right opportunities and with very little forethought end up having a great career.

Others…not so much. Many people end up plateauing senselessly, getting stuck in a rut. Or worse, some find themselves at a dead end in a company they hate, doing a job they loathe or going down a career path they don't want.

Once this happens it's hard to turn back, switch course or hit the reset button. You've got time and money invested in what you are doing. You've got kids, mortgages and responsibilities.

When this happens, too many people start to die inside, little by little. If this is you, then please, heed the advice below because…

Life is too short to have a career you don't
ABSOLUTELY LOVE!

And it's easier than you think, if you're brave enough to ask yourself the right questions on a regular basis and take appropriate actions to course correct.

If this is one of your staff members, then you have an employee who is neither engaged nor doing their best work. And you owe it to both the employee and you to have these discussions.

The good news is that whether this is you or one of your staff, you can fix it — or help them to do so — as long as you keep a few things in mind.

1. We work to live; we don't live to work. Your professional goals need to be congruent with your personal ones. If not, your career trajectory is not sustainable.

2. The smallest things can make the biggest difference. Even if you hate your job now, as long as you loved it in the first place it probably won't take much for you to fall in love with it all over again.

3. Sometimes the ability to pick yourself up and dust yourself off after a setback can make or break your chances of achieving your goals. There is a lot to be said for resilience.

We will look at each of these in turn, but first let's talk about why managers might be afraid to have these conversations with staff.

Why Managers Don't Talk to Staff about Their Careers

In fact, many managers avoid this topic like the plague for one of several reasons:

- They themselves don't understand how to manage their own careers and are hesitant to talk to their employees about theirs.
- They are afraid that if they help their staff better manage their careers they will surpass them on the corporate ladder.
- They are afraid to talk about career development because they don't feel they can meet the employee's expectations, or that staff expectations may differ from what the manager would like to see staff do. This is especially true in smaller companies or niche functions where there is not a lot of vertical career opportunity available.
- The staff that they manage are very senior in their careers and they feel ill-equipped to help someone older or more senior than themselves.
- The staff members in question are Critical People and the manager feels that they are very focused and goal oriented, therefore they are not only capable of managing their careers without the manager's assistance but are probably already doing so.

Let's address these in turn. We will talk about the basic mechanics of career management a bit later so we will skip the first point for now. And we've already addressed the last point in Chapter 3, where we highlighted the need to spend 80 percent of your time working with your Critical People.

Addressing the second point, if you yourself manage your career well, you'll never have to worry about being surpassed. Good managers are typically well recognized for developing staff, so proper career management for both you and your staff is truly in your best interest. In fact, many companies are now measuring managers on their ability to develop staff for further opportunities.

Helping your staff manage their careers makes good business sense. Helping them understand what opportunities exist within your company (something they may not recognize without your help) will deter them from looking outside, saving you the time, expense and frustration of having to replace them.

But how do we address the third point? If you work in a small company or department, there just may not be that many opportunities to move up the career ladder. Or what if your aspirations for your staff members differ from their own?

Many managers are afraid of highlighting these limited or differing career opportunities. The assumption here is that all staff are interested in vertical career development — climbing that corporate ladder, if you will. But as we've already discussed, that simply isn't true. Many people want to manage career around family or simply want to do interesting work in a good company with people they like.

But all staff want to learn, grow and develop horizontally. Experience tells us that if you help them do that and honestly address their career aspirations (even if they differ from your own), they become very loyal and they actually look for reasons to stay instead of opportunities to leave.

You may not be able to stop them from eventually leaving, but you could certainly delay the inevitable. And if they leave in these circumstances instead of being frustrated or annoyed with their lack of career opportunities, you will have an ally instead of a detractor. Who knows? They may even help you find their replacement.

And what about those more senior staff? Shouldn't they have their careers figured out already? The short answer is no. As we've seen above, many never learn to manage their careers well, regardless of their age.

Three Generations — One Conversation

But let's talk a moment about helping people from the different generations. There are three generations currently in the workforce. The Gen Y's (also known as Millennials) are the youngest generation and are currently in their early 30's. Gen Xers are between their early 30's and late 40's/early 50's. And finally, Baby Boomers currently span their early 50's to retirement age.

It should be obvious why managers should have career development conversations with the youngest generation — the Gen Y's. But what about the other two generations? Quite simply, these conversations need to be had with *all* generations because people's priorities change over time.

The Gen Xers — even those who were highly motivated and driven to climb the corporate ladder — may start to re-evaluate when they begin to settle down and raise families. When their personal priorities begin to shift you might need to help them shift their professional ones as well, at least for a period of time.

And we are seeing Baby Boomers retire quite differently than former generations. The days of quitting work at age 65 and spending the rest of your life playing golf are becoming a thing of the past. Many Boomers continue to work long past the age of 65 because they are healthy and still want to contribute. They would become bored if they only spent their days on the golf course, working in the garage, doing craftwork or other hobbies.

Others of this generation can't afford to stop working, either because of poor planning or bad financial returns resulting from the financial crisis of 2007–2008.

Whatever the reason, more and more of our workforce will soon be approaching or past retirement age, and they need help not only planning for their future but also entering into this new paradigm — one where retirement isn't automatic at age 65 — with as little stress and angst as possible.

What Is the Career Development Conversation?

So, we need to talk to all of our staff about their careers. But what do we actually talk about? Let's go back to the points above and discuss each one.

#1: We Work to Live; We Don't Live to Work.

Or we *shouldn't* live to work. A healthy Social Age workplace honors and celebrates people's personal goals. If you have employees who live to work, keep an eye on them: it's typically not a happy life and they will run the risk of burnout.

The vast majority of us work to live, and therefore our professional goals must support our personal ones. If they don't, ultimately employees will become unhappy and leave (or be forced to leave by their spouse or family).

Therefore, the first rule in proactive career management is to *ensure that personal and professional goals are aligned.*

A word of caution here: *you do not need to know what your employees' personal goals are.* They are *personal.* Some of your staff will be happy to share them with you, and some of you reading this book will have the relationship with your staff that is conducive to this. Others, however, won't want to share, and some managers won't want to know. That's okay. The point is that as a manager you need to encourage your staff to think about and write down their personal goals.

It's a good idea to do these exercises yourself prior to working with your staff. Let's work through these from both a personal perspective as well as a scenario where you are working with your staff.

There are, of course many ways to set goals. Here is a simple yet comprehensive one adapted from Goal-Setting-for-Success.com.

Setting Personal Goals

1. If you were given $1 million tax-free how would you spend it? List at least ten items you would buy. These could be tangible items (new car or house) or intangible like going on trips (have you always wanted to see France?) or having experiences (sky diving?).

2. It's three years into the future and you run into a long-lost friend whom you haven't seen in all that time. You go for coffee and catch up and they ask about your life. The last three years have been your best yet! You're extremely proud of what you've accomplished. You tell your friend...

   - I live...
   - I earn my living by... (if you don't know the job title, write down how you spend your time at work)
   - I earn $X per year!
   - I spend my free time...
   - I have (gotten married, divorced, started dating, had children).
   - I've taken up...
   - I've given up...
   - I've learned...

3. You've just been given $100,000 to donate to one charity. Which one would you give it to?

4. Complete the following statements. The last time I:

    - Felt successful was...

    - Did something that I really didn't want to do (but felt great about doing) was...

    - Felt truly happy was...

    - Felt truly at peace was...

    - Felt really proud of myself was...

    - Felt totally focused was...

    - Was told I did a great job was...

    - Developed a new skill was...

5. You have won the lottery and never have to worry about money again. You can work if you choose to, but don't have to if you don't want to. How would you spend your days?

These questions will help you define long- and short-term goals and cover everything from tangible toys you'd like to acquire, experiences you would like to have, contributions you'd like to make, who you'd like to spend your time with and how you'd like to spend your days at work and at play.

Can you think of anything these questions missed? Jot those down too.

Comparing Professional Goals to Personal Ones

Now that you have identified your personal goals it's time to compare them with your professional goals. Write down your professional goals for the next one to three years. Why this time frame? Because that's about as far around the corner as we can see in these very dynamic times. So do this exercise on a yearly basis, always looking at a one- to three-year rolling time frame.

Now compare the two lists and ask yourself, *How synchronized/harmonized are these two sets of goals?* Rate each of your professional goals on a scale of 1 to 10. A rating of 1 means the professional goal is not congruent with or does not support your personal goals. A rating of 10 means the two are completely aligned and the professional goal perfectly supports achieving your personal goals.

Note: To do this you want to take each professional goal *individually* and compare it with *all of your personal goals as a whole.*

A Personal/Professional Goals Case Study

Camilla was an IT project manager who engaged Deborah, a career coach, to help her change jobs. *"I want to retrain. I hate my job. I've just come back from working overseas and I'm going to take this opportunity to retrain and do something that I absolutely love."* She thought that what she would absolutely love to do was to become a chef.

Deborah started working with Camilla as she did with all her career-coaching clients — by helping her define her personal goals.

Camilla was a 32-year-old single female without children. Guess what her top two personal goals were? You guessed it: to find a husband and have children. Now think about a chef's life. Do they work a 9 to 5 job? Typically, no. They work crazy hours and lots of them.

So it was fairly obvious to Deborah that Camilla's personal goals were not congruent with her professional ones. Had she retrained as a chef, she would have been even more miserable than she was.

Deborah's solution? She helped Camilla to identify what she originally liked about the work she did and where she did it. It turned out that she actually loved the work but was working for a very male-dominated company with very few females. She felt marginalized to the point that her self-confidence had started to wane. This made her start to think about leaving. But not just making a small change — making an enormous one and training into a completely different field.

Camilla found a job back in her hometown, as an IT Project Manager, but it was with a company in an industry she was passionate about — healthcare. It was also with a company where she felt very much at home: accepted and supported.

And her thoughts of becoming a chef are a distant memory.

Now look at your ratings. Identify any professional goals that you rated less than a 6 or 7. For these goals you want to challenge the reason why you set the goal (or why your staff member has set this as a professional goal).

The first question is to ask yourself (or them) is why? Is this your idea or someone else's — for example do you want to become a lawyer because *you* want to become a lawyer or because your mother is one? Does this professional goal really excite you, or do you feel like it's an obligation?

Note: This question is especially relevant when working with staff, even when their professional and personal goals are aligned. You want to make sure that they are not just giving you a set of professional goals that *they think you want to hear.*

For instance, take two real-life responses to the goal-setting question. These conversations occurred during a coaching session where an Ignite Global consultant was working with a manager, Steve, on having one-on-one Career Development Conversations with his staff.

Both staff members were asked about their professional goals and both responded, "I want to go into management."

Interestingly Steve's number one priority at that time was succession planning. So he became really excited when both of his top two people told him they wanted to step into his shoes.

But the consultant slowed the conversations down and asked, "Why"?

The first young engineer replied, "Because I love being able to pass along a skill to somebody. And I love to see people succeed, grow and get better." She then went on to describe how she spent her weekends at a surf beach teaching surf life saving and certifying the beach patrol. Her eyes lit up and she became very animated talking about what a buzz she got when she saw someone, especially someone who may have been struggling through her course, pass it.

The second staff member however struggled to answer the why question. He stumbled around with no clarity about the real reason for wanting the promotion. Upon further good-natured probing, the consultant discovered that this young man's only real career goal at this time was to work for a company that allowed him the flexibility to take time off to travel. And that's fine, because this company was just such a company. They were happy to let him work for most of the year and then to let him take extended time off to travel because they were getting great value from his work while he was there.

Neither career goals were a problem for Steve. But he could have spent a lot of time and resources (financial and otherwise) unnecessarily giving these two young professionals the same opportunity to grow into a management position. The young man's career goals may change in a few years and he could eventually become a successful manager. But at this stage in his life he's really not even thinking about it.

The young woman, however, is another story. She is truly someone you'd want to back for a management position, because she wants it for the right reasons and she's ready for it. She's not just telling Steve what he wants to hear.

It is important to challenge your staff on their professional goals and find out the underlying reasons behind why they think they make sense. If you do this early and often, you will more than likely avoid a lot of pain and heartache by channeling resources in the right areas and by appropriately managing expectations.

When Is It Okay for Professional and Personal Goals NOT to Align?

If you honestly feel happy in your job right now, but are aghast to realize that none or very few of your professional goals are in line with your personal ones, don't worry! *If it ain't broke, don't fix it.* You can be both happy professionally and personally and have seemingly incongruent goals. Why? There are probably more reasons than these, but here are two that we find frequently come up in our workshops.

First, you may see your personal and professional goals as being completely separate (i.e. you might be someone who is passionate about running marathons and does not see how any professional goals could align with that goal). In this instance, one of your main professional goals might be to have a job that allows the flexibility you need to train, or provides the financial resources that allow you to travel to compete. As long as you're in a job that allows you this flexibility and checks off your other Currencies of Choice, you may be quite happy.

Similarly, you may be a working parent who has taken a step backwards or sideways in your career to allow you to dedicate more time to family. Your current professional goals might give you the additional time or reduced stress to allow you to focus on your home life.

If this is the case, you simply need to think beyond your child raising years and try to determine where you would like to go from that point on (both personally and professionally). Then set goals that make sure you keep yourself on track while you are taking this step back for the eventual return to the "career ladder."

#2: Sometimes the Smallest Things Can Make the Biggest Difference.

Remember the concept of throwing the baby out with the bathwater? We do that far too frequently as human beings. It's a natural reaction. Especially in today's instant gratification society, when we become upset or frustrated most of us don't stop to think about how we could just modify a few little things to help us get over our frustration or to become happy again. Instead we think, *I'm unhappy, I need to make a change.* And when we do this many of the changes we make are big changes, like leaving a spouse, or a job.

But sometimes — in fact, many times — the smallest things *can* make the biggest difference.

Remember, usually we don't take a job unless we think we'll like it. We'll like our boss, the team we work with, where we work and what we do. Yet, as time goes by some of the factors might change that made us love our jobs. Much of the time we don't even recognize that this is happening. The changes might be really subtle. We just know that something has changed and we no longer love our job, so we look for a new one.

But we don't have to make these big changes — and neither do your staff. In our work at Ignite Global, we have seen an incredible array of instances where top talent decided to stay in their current role because of something so small that it seemed like an impossibly simple fix. But the smallest change made all the difference. People have changed their minds about leaving because:

- They moved to another desk.
- They moved their desk around to face a different direction.
- They bought a light.
- They bought a new chair.
- They scheduled a 15-minute-per-week meeting with their manager.
- The company walled off a small area for a private lunchroom.
- The company bought plants and put them around the office.
- The company invested in training on the new, very difficult computer system making it easier to use and less frustrating.

- The company bought additional site licenses for software, increasing the number of users from 2 to 30 (and allowing multiple staff to use it without getting thrown off of it in the middle of a process).

- The company finally took employee complaints about the IT system and fixed it within a couple of months and for relatively little money.

- And the list goes on.

Impossible to believe? These are all true case studies of either individuals who were actively pursuing other jobs and decided to stay as a result of these changes, or of companies whose employee engagement scores went up as a result of these seemingly small changes.

A Small Changes Case Study

Allison was a paralegal at a law firm in a small town. She had been in this industry for 26 years and working at the same company for 17 years. Allison had never had a bad performance review.

Allison's husband heard Sue give a presentation on Career Management in their hometown and approached her after the session. "Can you help my wife?" he pleaded. "She needs to find another job; in fact she thinks she needs to go into a completely different field. She hates her job so much that it's giving her migraine headaches and she's had to miss a lot of work over the last year."

Allison paid for six sessions, but was refunded for all but two. Sue refunded her money because in the very first session Sue helped Allison fall in love with her job again. The second session was only to verify that the solutions they came up with worked.

Not only was Allison having migraines, it turned out that she had lost confidence in her ability to do her job. Again, this is a woman who had never had a bad performance review.

So what were the solutions? After seeing doctors for the previous year with no relief, Sue helped Allison recognize that the reason for her migraines was the fact that the law firm had moved offices a year earlier, around the time that the migraines started.

When questioned about her physical environment Allison commented that, "The only thing that really irritates me is that there's this light above me and it's just at the wrong angle. It's very bright and harsh.

Bright light and migraines: a possible connection? It turns out there was, because Allison simply had to move desks to make her migraines disappear.

But what about her loss of confidence? Allison, it turns out, was very motivated by external praise (see the Underlying Motivators Conversation).

In the old office environment, she sat right next to her manager. Because they were in close proximity and he was very free to give praise, she had a constant stream of positive feedback. But in the new office he was on a completely different floor and she barely saw him.

Allison realized that she missed the pats on the back and not having them made her question her abilities. To fix this issue, she simply scheduled a 15-minute weekly meeting with her manager. Problem solved.

How do you find out what small changes can make the biggest difference in your staff's lives? You ask them, of course.

And this is where the Career Development and the Feedback Conversations collide. In order to determine what little things can decrease your employees' frustrations and increase their engagement levels, you need to be willing to ask some questions that could be a bit confronting for you as a manager. Questions like:

- *What irritates or frustrates you about how I manage you?*
- *How do you feel about your relationship with me? Do you need more of my time? Less?*
- *Do I give you too much autonomy or flexibility or not enough?*
- *Do I micro-manage you?*
- *What else would you like from me?*

But it's not only questions about you as their manager that you want to ask; it's also questions about their team, like:

- *How do you get along with your team?*
- *How well do you work together?*
- *What frustrates you about your team dynamics?*
- *Do you socialize with them? If not, is that important?*

You also will want to ask them about the work they do, but that falls under the Feedback and Objectives Conversations.

And yes, finally you do want to ask questions about their physical work environment — their chair, their desk, the lighting in the office, the office space, the location, even the air they breathe. Some of these questions will seem silly to you, but try it: you will be shocked and amazed at the things they say. And equally shocked and amazed at how easy it is to make a difference in someone's attitude by making a small change like a plant, chair or lunch room.

#3: *Help Them Build Resilience.*

The third and final concept in the Career Development Conversation is resilience. This is an important conversation to have with all staff, but particularly important with the youngest generation, the Gen Y's or Millennials.

Research is showing that Millennials are not particularly adept at overcoming setbacks. Remember, this is the generation who got a trophy in school just for participating. Many times they don't know how to react to constructive criticism, a lost promotion, a project going wrong, etc., simply because they have never faced anything like it. We could get angry about this, or we could recognize it for what it is and simply help them.

But it's not only the youngest generation that needs help in overcoming setbacks from time to time. All of us experience very difficult personal hardships from time to time, like illness, death, separation or missed opportunities. And sometimes we can make rash decisions when we are not thinking clearly. We're like pinballs being bounced from the obstacle into completely different and unpredictable trajectories.

This is why building resilience is so important. Sometimes you can help your staff by just being there to talk to them (again, this is part of the Feedback Conversation). Sometimes you might have to help them seek help. Or, you could invest in resilience training.

However you choose to handle this as a manager, the most important point is that you need to talk to them about what's going on — which is a good lead-in to the last section in this chapter, how to hold the Career Development Conversation.

A Resilience Case Study

John, the Controller of a large pharmaceutical company, was one of those people who never had to have a resume. He was great at his job and kept getting tapped on the shoulder for one position after another.

Until the recession hit and John lost his job. (To be fair, he was offered another, which he declined because it would have meant a relocation.)

But he wasn't worried. After all, he'd never had to look for a job — they always found him. However, this time John was out of work for 18 months, and this devastated him. He finally took a contract role with a marketing firm, helping them install a new computer system in the finance department. It was boring work at a much lower level than John had been used to. After 18 months he found the contract work, and his life, soul-destroying.

Today, the economy has recovered in the area where he lives and there are frequent positions that he would be quite suitable for advertised on the local job boards. All of his peers affected by the downturn have found work, but John is still at this contract role, now several years on. He's waiting for his next job to come to him.

John did not have the resilience to rebound from such a setback. He still hasn't reconciled the fact in his own mind that he needs to pursue opportunities because the days of them coming to him are long over.

How to Hold the Career Development Conversation

The Career Development Conversation should be one of the easiest conversations you will have. After all, who *doesn't* want to talk about their career and where they want to go? Well, there will be a few people, but their number should be relatively small.

Remember, the components of this conversation are to:

- Ensure their professional goals are aligned with and support their personal ones
- Ensure their professional goals are truly their own and that they are positively motivated about achieving them for the right reasons
- Determine what if anything about their job, their manager (you), their team or their work environment is frustrating them and how these frustrations can be fixed
- Help them build resilience to overcome setbacks

In order to do that you will first need to talk about why you want to have conversations with them about their career and helping them to proactively manage it. For that you can use the following Conversation Starters.

Conversation Starters

- *Today I'd like to talk a bit about your career development. I really want to make sure that we work together to help you achieve your goals because the happier you are at work, the more productive you'll be and the better your relationship with the entire team will be.*

- *I'd like to talk a bit about your personal goals. Do you do goal setting? If so, do you write them down? Tell me a bit about your process. (Again, your aim is not to find out what their personal goals are — you just want to ensure whether or not they are congruent with their professional goals.)*

- *Where do you see yourself in the company or industry within three to five years?*

  - *Why? (Make sure it's for the right reasons, not to live up to someone else's expectations or because they think it's what you want to hear.)*

- *What steps do you need to take to get there? (This should form the basis of an action plan.)*

- *How would you rate these statements, from most to least important?*

  - *I want to climb as far as I can on the career ladder.*

  - *I want to successfully manage work around family.*

  - *I want to do interesting work with people I like at a company I can back.*

- *Do you see yourself managing staff? Why or why not? (Make sure it's for the right reasons, not to live up to someone else's expectations.)*

- *If you could move into any other department or function, where would you move and why?*

- *Are there additional responsibilities or projects you'd like to take on? Why?*

- *What can we do to help you grow professionally?*

- *I'd like to talk to you about what's frustrating you about your job. Sometimes the smallest things can make the biggest difference, and I'd really like to find out what, if anything, is driving you to distraction about me, your team, your work environment or anything else.*

- *You seem a bit (down, distracted, impatient…) lately. Is everything all right? Has anything happened I need to be aware of?*

- *I know that (fill in the blank) has recently happened. How are you doing with it?*

Review Professional Goals and Incorporate Them into Their Job Objectives

Once your begin the conversations with them you can encourage them to set personal goals (if they haven't yet) and then move to the professional goal conversation. Are these professional goals aligned with, and do they support, their personal goals? If not, why not? Remember to challenge them to make sure that the professional goals are truly their own and that they are set for the right reasons.

Word of warning: If they tell you they have professional goals that you don't feel are achievable or will take them in the wrong direction, you will need to have open, honest conversations with them about that. But be careful not to impose unfair limitations on them. The surest way to help someone fail is by telling them they will. Instead of telling them they can't, if you sincerely believe this, help them to reach this conclusion for themselves. Who knows — they just may surprise you!

Once their professional goals are aligned with your expectations, incorporate them into their job objectives (see the chapter on the Objectives Conversation) and work with them to create an action plan to achieve these goals and objectives.

You can also use this as a basis for professional development and training.

Help Them Fall in Love with Their Job Again and Build Resilience

We have already talked about how to have these conversations with your staff. Helping them to fall in love with their job again is simply a matter of asking the questions in the section above and then fixing the issues or managing their expectations.

And the only way to help them build resilience is to monitor what's going on with them (either through observation or by using the Conversation Starters above) and help them the best way you know how.

Conclusion

As you can see, the Career Development Conversation fits nicely with both the Feedback and the Objectives Conversations. With this conversation, you can help your staff to better manage their careers at every stage of life. When your staff become more focused on what they want to achieve professionally, and when you assist them by providing the training and development they need to achieve their goals, staff will become more productive while you build greater "bench strength" within your team. Helping staff with their career goals also builds loyalty and trust, as your staff perceive you as someone who supports them in reaching both their personal and professional goals.

Putting It into Action:
First Steps from This Chapter

As you begin to roll the Career Development, Underlying Motivators and Strengths Conversations into your monthly meetings, remember, Rome wasn't built in a day. Take each of these conversations in bite-sized chunks. For guidance on how to schedule each of the conversations and exercises throughout a calendar year download the *FOCUSed* Conversations Planner at http://igniteglobal. com/mrfmbook/.

1. Use the Conversation Starters to introduce the Career Development Conversation.

2. Encourage them to set their personal goals.

3. Ask them (alone or with your assistance depending on the level) to set professional goals.

4. Once agreed, incorporate these professional goals into their job objectives.

5. Have them (alone or with your assistance depending on the level of employee) develop action plans to achieve these goals.

6. Help them fall in love with their job again by determining what frustrates them. Fix these issues or manage their expectations.

7. Help them build resilience.

Notes

7 | *FOCUSed* Conversation #4:

The Underlying Motivators Conversation

© iStock/skodonnell

The Underlying Motivators Conversation at a Glance

1. Helps you to determine what your staff need to be motivated to "go the extra mile."
2. Helps you to understand how your staff want to be recognized and rewarded.

Why It's Important

It goes without saying that productivity and effectiveness increase in direct proportion to motivation — that is, as long as you've hired the right people and they are in the right roles. But this has become one of the most confusing and frustrating areas of employee management.

Most managers intuitively know that their staffs need to be motivated. They also know that different people respond to different types of motivation. But how do they figure out what each individual needs or will respond to? And how much responsibility does the manager need to take to motivate their staff versus the staff taking responsibility for their own motivation?

Confusing topics to be sure — which is why the Underlying Motivators Conversation is critical.

Let's accept that people who are engaged with their responsibilities and work in an environment that fosters engagement get better results. Let's also accept that if someone's work and their work environment helps them to feel good about themselves and what they're doing, their motivation and engagement will increase.

To accomplish this, we need to dig down past the obvious stereotypes about motivation to uncover people's real underlying motivators — those that can truly unlock potential and unleash productivity. This chapter will show you how to do both, and how to avoid traps that continue to hold many organizations back. It will also give you the tools and help you be confident in putting them to good use. The results of this conversation are as follows:

- Employees will accelerate their progress towards the right objectives.

- You will set up the conditions that foster innovation and creativity, allowing employees to be more strategic and solutions-oriented.

- You as a manager will free up time for other activities that will enable you to better achieve your goals; you'll spend less time trying to fix "motivators" that don't work.

- Your team and your organization will benefit through better short-term and long-term results.

An Old Paradigm Rears Its Ugly Head

So much of what we thought we knew about people's underlying motivators is based on an approach that used to work, but that has lost much of its relevance. If we don't understand why that is so, we'll be condemned to repeat the same mistakes over and over.

So let's start by discovering:

- When and why things went wrong in motivation at work
- How some partial fixes were found, but why they are unsatisfactory
- Which insights into motivation to take with you into the new era

We will then explore:

- Two recent key models that can dramatically improve this situation
- How to have an Underlying Motivators Conversation

A Change We Never Saw Coming

As we've already seen, work has changed a lot over the past few decades. In the previous Industrial Age, gaining and keeping employment was often a matter of showing how well you could perform set sequences of actions and stick to the rules. Those rules were often printed out in a manual or on a large poster on a wall. Flexibility was zero or close to it. Efficiency was the name of the game. Most employees weren't paid to think, just to do. The more you did, the more you earned. That was how motivation worked in the Industrial Age.

The name often associated with this era is Frederick Winslow Taylor, an American mechanical engineer. Taylor made a sizable contribution to the "Time and Motion" movement as the 19th century was coming to an end, in which employee activity was studied and broken down into component parts. These activity components were then optimized to give the best manual output for the least time spent, because at the time, that's what business success was all about.

A Deep-Rooted Mindset

But Taylor wasn't the first to beat the drum about optimizing labor and tasks in production. The roots of this idea run deep, and so do the notions of motivation that go with it. To see why so many managers in the last few years have been blind-sided, confused and frustrated, rewind another hundred-plus years, back to Adam Smith, the Scottish philosopher and author of *The Wealth of Nations*. Smith used the example of a pin factory. When workers each tried to accomplish the whole process of producing a pin, output was meager; but when each worker specialized in just one part of the process, output could grow a hundredfold.

We've had over two hundred years of the pin factory "division of labor" model in business and its approach to motivation, and it isn't over yet. There's a good reason why this model continues — because it still works for mass production, and we still mass produce many things.

Adapt or Die (Version 1.0)

Here's an important point, however: as machines have been designed with more and more capabilities and intelligence, they have increasingly replaced direct employee intervention in production environments. Similarly, computer software has gotten smarter as well. Companies run online sales operations where the whole process of advertising, attracting, convincing, taking payment from and delivering to customers is automated via different e-commerce systems. Each part of the process is studied and optimized, certainly; but now more of those parts are performed directly by machines or systems, and less are performed by human beings.

Did organizations and managers see those work activity changes coming? Yes, for the most part, they did. If not, they suffered loss of revenue, market share and profitability. Some enterprises fell by the wayside, unable to adapt, but mostly (and sometimes with groans) organizations adapted their work activities to suit.

"Rejiggering" the Workforce

Where does that leave the workforce? Much of the manual effort is no longer required because automation can do the same tasks faster, better and without lunch breaks. But at the same time, other major changes are also afoot. Customers have discovered that they now have the power. Instead of the manufacturer-driven demand of a few decades ago, markets are now being defined by what customers want instead of what manufacturers deign to offer them.

Organizations (and that includes both private businesses and public services) now have to figure out how to better mesh with customer demand, pin factory or no pin factory. To do that, they now have to pay their employees not just to do, but also (gasp) to think!

The bottom line is, the old command and control structures are inadequate for the new demand-driven, web-enabled era. Throw increased competition through globalization into the mix and you have one heady cocktail.

The smart money is now on the *customer-oriented organization,* where customer-facing employees make decisions in real time about how best to satisfy those customers, instead of handing the decision up the management chain and waiting for the response (by which time the customer has found another supplier over the web anyway).

Motivation: Lost in Translation?

So much for the changes in activity, responsibility and thinking. But what about *motivation?* Unlike production activity and sales figures, motivation is a more slippery, difficult to quantify factor that does not always show up where you'd expect it. Nonetheless, motivation and engagement are huge factors in the overall success of a company. Unfortunately, too many organizations, while recognizing the importance of employee motivation, haven't made the transition from the approach to motivation that worked in the age of the pin factory to what works for employees today.

This is the change that we never saw coming. We've transformed our manufacturing models, we've flipped our business processes upside down and we've turned our marketing inside out. But we've neglected to *modernize our approach to the one thing that drives all of this: employee motivation.*

It's here that this Underlying Motivators Conversation chapter really starts: with the realization that we now need to undo an attitude that has lasted for a couple of centuries and get back to a few simple truths about the underlying motivators of people working in our organization.

Motivation Mania

"Motivation? I learned all about that in business school!"

I bet you did! The question is, what kind of motivation did you learn about — and is it still applicable? There is no shortage of ideas and preconceptions flying around on the subject. Let's look at some of the limiting concepts that have often been handed out with the best intentions in the world and some of the least positive effects.

- *"I can motivate you."* In fact, no, I can't. You are the only person who can motivate you. As Robert Townsend, author of *Up the Organization,* once remarked, motivation is a door that is locked from the inside. What a manager can do, however, is to find out from you what your motivations are and create an environment that supports those motivations. This is the basis of the *Locus of Motivation* tool and the *Motivators Continuum* we'll see further on.

- *Carrots and sticks.* In this approach, if I want you to perform better, I'll offer you a reward if you reach a certain standard of performance. Alternatively, to avoid poor performance or failure I'll threaten you with unpleasant consequences if your performance falls below a certain level. A key point about carrots and sticks is that they are offered or imposed before you perform: this is also a key failing in their effectiveness, because this system actually narrows our focus. In the Industrial Age, this failing was disguised by the particular nature of the performance to be achieved (manual productivity). But today that failing is out in the open and it's getting ugly. We need to broaden our focus to achieve the more innovative, strategic and creative work required in the Social Age. Traditional carrots and sticks work well when the work is routine, tactical and predictable, but fails miserably when even a modicum of cognitive ability is required.

- *"Just push the right buttons."* Because it recognizes that different people have different buttons and takes individual personality into account, this is a big step forward from the "one carrot (or stick) fits all" approach. But while I might be able to push buttons somewhere to create the right environment, I can't push your buttons because that's your privilege and yours alone.

- *The guilt trip.* A primitive tool based on rudimentary notions of psychology, "laying a guilt trip" on someone can have varying effects. However, the positive ones are short-term at best. Suggesting to someone that he or she is "letting the side down" or saying, "C'mon, you're better than this!" may work in crisis situations. But crisis situations are (hopefully) not normal situations, and motivation skills should function in all situations, not just the desperate ones.

- *The hiring choice: intelligence or enthusiasm?* Many hiring managers have learned (often from bitter personal experience) that if they have to choose between a candidate who is smart and a candidate who is enthusiastic, enthusiasm is the better bet. You may find yourself having to count to ten sometimes if your motivated-but-not-quite-so-bright employee doesn't "get it" the first time around. By comparison however, intelligence without enthusiasm in the workplace is a cancer.

   Enthusiasm and underlying motivators still need to be tended to after onboarding has finished. Even robust plants wither and die if they don't get the right light, food and water. The good news is that by adopting a suitable approach to those underlying motivators, you can get both intelligence *and* enthusiasm.

Do any of the points above look, well, a little too familiar? If so, take heart. Some of the most prominent leaders have made mistakes about motivation. A superb business magazine cartoon about Margaret Thatcher when she was the prime minister struggling with Britain's economy showed her sitting on a donkey (which was British business), dangling a stick on a string in front of the donkey's head — and beating it from behind with a carrot.

Which Model Should You Use for Motivation?

"All models are wrong, but some are useful."[25] When statistician George E.P. Box made this statement, he was thinking about using mathematics to model reality. However, it's true in general. By definition, a model will never contain everything that there is in reality — or else it would be reality, and no longer a model!

Especially for something as complex as personality, a model or technique is best viewed as a support to help you apply your own judgment and common sense to get the best results. That's true of the 5 *FOCUSed*

Conversations and of the Underlying Motivators Conversation as well.

What is surprising, given the infinite subtlety of personalities, is that the old carrot and stick model, the crudest motivation model of all, has been so popular for so long. The reason for this is important enough to bear repeating. As Daniel Pink pointed out in *Drive,* the old rewards motivation model worked for manual production and the output of tangible goods or services.[26] It wasn't necessarily the best model to use, but in the Industrial Age, there wasn't much else, and overall, companies did better by using it.

What Is the Underlying Motivators Conversation?

When a new management model or fad comes along, there is often a knee-jerk reaction to throw out the old models. However, many bright people have studied motivation in the past and come up with valuable insights. If no model can truly represent reality, there may be no point in trashing one partially correct view, only to replace it with another partially correct one. You may be better off combining both.

The Underlying Motivators Conversation should therefore do two things. It should give you a solid platform from which to work if the topic of motivators is new to you. And it should also build on any valid knowledge about motivators that you may already have.

For example, let's take the Hierarchy of Needs defined by Abraham Maslow in 1943.[27] Maslow's model suggests that a person's basic needs (including food, water and shelter) must be satisfied first. When these needs are met, but not before, then the person successively seeks to belong, to be esteemed and finally to become whatever that person believes he or she should be ("self-actualization"). All this made sense when Maslow defined it and it still does.

Or consider the Two-Factor Theory (Motivation-Hygiene Theory) put forward by Frederick Herzberg in 1964.[28] Herzberg observed that money (as in a salary or wages) is something an employee can't do without — but that if you keep piling on more money and more bonuses, it doesn't necessarily lead to better performance.

So as you now start to find out about the Locus of Motivation, the Motivators Continuum, and the Autonomy-Mastery-Purpose (AMP) model from Daniel Pink, keep in mind valid insights from the past too. You'll see how the Underlying Motivators Conversation builds on these classics and adds to them in a wholly useful and practical way.

Scientific Approaches

There have been a number of intriguing scientific experiments (with sponsors including the Federal Reserve no less) carried out to see how money or external remuneration affects performance. It turns out that offering more money for better performance only really works in situations where the work to be done is "algorithmic." That means the employee proceeds according to fixed rules; speed and accuracy are the most important factors. This model fits Industrial Age work well.[29]

However, when creativity and innovation (the hallmarks of the Social Age) become more important, money and bonuses start to lose their impact. In fact, people even start to do worse when offered bigger performance bonuses than people offered much smaller performance bonuses!

There are different explanations for why this should be so. The theory of cognitive dissonance provides one. It says that people who don't get the bonus but who are asked to do the work need to rationalize why they are doing it. Because there is no material incentive, they decide that the job itself must be worth doing ("It's not for the money").

They attach importance to the job itself and make bigger efforts to do it well. Without financial bonuses or other perks, the motivators must come from elsewhere. Two very big motivators are *Internal Challenge* and *External Praise*.

The Locus of Motivation: Internal Challenge or External Praise?

Have you ever wondered why some people just don't respond to praise? Or worse, they respond negatively to it? Or they do a great job but are really uncomfortable with you telling them, "Nice job"? Have you ever tried (and failed) to motivate someone by egging them on to do a better job, or even by having them compete in some way with a co-worker? Have you wondered why these tactics work for some people and not for others? And how you can figure out which works for whom?

This is because each of us has a different *Locus of Motivation*. Your employees sit somewhere on the continuum between two extremes. At one extreme are people who are motivated exclusively by challenging themselves to do better and better. They are the people who say, "I see a mountain, I'm going to climb that mountain just to prove to myself that I can." They don't really care what other people think (and sometimes respond even negatively to praise). These employees are centered on *Internal Challenge*.

At the other extreme are people who are motivated by doing well in front of others. They are the ones that will only climb the mountain if they know you will recognize and reward them for it. They typically hate competition and will shy away from anything that looks like competition, unless they know they can win. These employees are oriented towards *External Praise*.

Ignite Global has developed the Locus of Motivation exercise as a practical tool to help managers understand how they themselves function, and how they can better understand the motivators for the people in their teams.

Try the following quick exercise for yourself to see how Internal Challenge and External Praise characteristics might apply for you.

Are you motivated to do a better job when you:

- Have set a BHAG (big, hairy, audacious goal) for yourself?

- Are competing against your own past performance or against your co-workers or peers' performances?

- Know that you will get praise or recognition from someone?

- Hope to be better thought of or accepted by your manager, team, your customers or external stakeholders?

Locus of Motivation Case Study

Kate was a good recruiter. Her clients respected her and her candidates loved her. And she was successful, regularly appearing near the top of the regional score card or league table. But she did just enough to be respected, never really striving for the top spot. In her mind, as long as she was beating her results from the previous month and the previous year, that was enough.

One night Kate and her team were out to dinner with their boss and the Regional Manager, Dave. Kate had just started a new division in the office. She loved the challenge of building something from the ground up and had no real goals for the year other than to put a respectable amount of revenue "on the board."

Dave knew Kate needed a challenge. Dave also needed the revenue for his region. So, sometime between the main course and dessert, Dave leaned in to Kate and said quietly, "You are a force of nature. I really think that you could build this division to be number one in the region for the year."

Kate was incredulous. She would be competing against recruiters in the region servicing bigger markets with much more tenure and a much larger client base. She would be competing with offices that had had this particular division up and running for over a decade.

But Dave "threw down the gauntlet" and Kate picked it up.

The very large glass trophy that recognizes Kate's achievement for being the top recruiter in the region for that division sits on the bookcase in her home office to this day.

The Motivators Continuum

Remember what we said above about the "push the right buttons" approach? While it sets the scene for understanding how different people respond to their environment in different ways, it might be interpreted as suggesting people themselves are "push-button" objects. We know this doesn't work.

Moreover, buttons are either "on" or "off." This doesn't work for people either. Just like your weight doesn't jump up or down by five pounds, neither does your enthusiasm to do a particular job. Whether it's high or low, it got to where it is by following a continuous curve. The Motivators Continuum takes account of the fact that we lean in greater or lesser degrees towards different motivators, without necessarily being either fully "on" or "off."

As a practical way to find your Locus of Motivation, in Ignite Global's manager training sessions you answer a series of carefully designed, straightforward questions. Each question has two possible answers. One is the answer that somebody with a very high Internal Challenge motivation would give; on the other side of the page is a corresponding answer that somebody with a very high External Praise motivation would give. Running between each such pair of answers is a Motivators Continuum scale from one to ten. You answer each question by indicating on the scale of one to ten which answer better reflects your personality.

For example:

Question:

When given praise, I respond more favorably to:

(Circle the number that best represents how you feel on the scale between the two extremes)

1   2   3   4   5   6   7   8   9   10

ANSWER A	ANSWER B
A private email or a quiet "well done" by my manager	Public acknowledgment in front of entire team or company (either in email or verbally)

Note: You can download the full Motivators Continuum Exercise at http://igniteglobal.com/mrfmbook/.

Author's Note: A Shout-Out to Leon

As founder and CEO of Ignite Global, I have regularly taught these conversations in management workshops since 2011. I developed the theory of the Locus of Motivation but had never really been happy with the way it helped managers recognize where their staff fell on the continuum. Until I met Leon.

Leon is a young manager working for an engineering firm. Not yet 30, Leon was in his first professional managerial role, although he had managed staff before within part-time and non-professional jobs.

Leon took this concept and ran with it. It helped him immediately better understand and support his own staff. But, being an engineer, he was dissatisfied with the rather ambiguous approach to determining which side of the continuum his staff favored.

During a group coaching facilitation Leon piped up and said,

"Kim, you have tools for everything you teach — you need to create one for this."

I replied, "I know, and I've been struggling to do just that, but I can't work it out."

Within five minutes Leon, the engineer, had mapped out a tool that could work. All I had to do was to construct the questions.

This is my shout-out to Leon, who is very much motivated by external recognition. Thank you!

But Still, What about the Money?

Even if numerous scientific experiments have shown how internal challenge and external praise can be far stronger motivators than money, it's not always easy to give up on a technique that has such a long history. And in some cases, you shouldn't give up on it — or at least, not entirely ignore it.

Let's explain. Money has the undeniable property of being quantifiable. A dollar is a dollar, and it's not 99 cents, even though the difference is relatively small. That means that one amount of money can be directly compared with another. That in turn means that money, besides being a means to acquire other things, is also a way of keeping score. For some people, this can be immensely important. Seeing the dollar figure on their paycheck and how it compares, for example, to how much they earned the previous month gives them immediate information about their performance.

In addition, many companies, especially the bigger ones, are measured every quarter on their financial performance. While enterprises need to have a long-term view and invest in people, technology and resources on that basis, they may never get to the long term if they don't make the numbers in the short term. And sometimes making the numbers calls for special incentives for salespeople, one of which may be more money for better sales performance *right now.*

Does this mean that money is the principal motivator for all sales-people? No, it doesn't. Salespeople may also be strongly motivated by a compulsion to be right, a need to prove they can make sales, or simply the desire to do a good job. They can be as sensitive to Internal Challenge and External Praise as any other employee.

But just as it's not a good idea to throw the baby out with the bathwater when it comes to models of motivation, it's not a good idea to try to completely remove money from the equation either. Just remember that while many employees will willingly focus on the job that needs doing as long as they are receiving reasonable remuneration, you may also meet one or two for whom money is quite simply the way they measure how well they are doing.

Daniel Pink's AMP: Autonomy, Mastery and Purpose

Daniel Pink, author of *Drive: The Surprising Truth About What Motivates Us,* has also produced a model to help better understand the people's underlying motivators. He states, "There is a disconnect between what science knows and what business does." He points out once again that *people are much more highly motivated by intrinsic factors — what we call "Currencies of Choice" — than by extrinsic ones such as remuneration.* Pink uses an elegant framework to describe these Underlying Motivators: *Autonomy, Mastery* and *Purpose.*

#1: Autonomy

Let's look first at autonomy and why people's drivers and motivators are different. Everyone is different and that's what makes people endlessly fascinating. That's also what makes managing people today so tough. No matter how innately good you are at it, it's one of the toughest jobs you'll ever have (other than raising children or herding cats).

People are driven by different things at different points in their lives, which is why we need to constantly have our finger on the pulse of our staff. The same person can be driven by different things at different points in time.

When Efficiency Trumped Autonomy

Over the last 20 to 30 years, it's been widely recognized that we need to treat individuals differently. Sure, we developed practices during the Industrial Revolution that we still use today to hire and manage people. Yet those practices were developed to manage a particular worker: someone who did very routine, repetitive, practical and predictable work.

Let's think back again to the factory floor during that time. One of the revolutionary things about it was how we developed a work force. We broke processes down to very specific things. So if we were making widgets on the factory floor, there would be one person responsible for making one part of the widget, another person responsible for making another part of the widget, and so on.

These tasks were organized in the way that lowered labor costs to a minimum. A worker would do the same thing over and over again. You didn't have to pay them a lot; they didn't have to be particularly bright and they were certainly discouraged from being innovative. Moreover, the factory floor operations were designed so that if one person was sick or on leave, someone else could easily take their place. Autonomy for a worker was not part of the deal.

It was easy to manage people back in the Industrial Age because it was a "one size fits all" management structure. We hired you to do one thing and you either did it well or you didn't. And if you didn't, you were out of there, right? This was a very dictatorial "command and control" model. No sitting down with your staff and saying, "How are things going? How's it going on the assembly line?"

Management Style Dinosaurs

Because this worked really well on the factory floor, we replicated those practices into the white collar and the professional world. This became the status quo. But with the dawn of the Social Age, everyone now needs to be more creative, strategic, and innovative and more solutions-oriented. So we demand autonomy from them in these areas. It's not a choice: it's an imposition.

The situation is driving managers crazy because they intuitively know that a one-size-fits-all approach to motivation no longer works. But they don't know what to do to tap into the individual's mind to figure out what does work. Managers can see the problem every day. What seems to work as a motivator for one person falls flat, or worse, acts as a de-motivator for another. Inspired guesses or luck gets managers out of some scrapes, but that's no way to build solid, dependable enthusiasm and results.

The New Work Models Are Based on Choice

If you grant autonomy rather than impose it, you give people a choice. If you have no choice you can feel trapped and disempowered. Conversely, when you have choice, you have options, the power to control your own destiny and freedom.

With the old Industrial Age paradigm, the working hours were 9 a.m. to 5 p.m. with no exception, regardless of whether there was a business reason for that or not. However, sometimes there are no compelling business reasons and we can set boundaries and parameters in a different way to offer autonomy that really is choice.

The littlest things make the biggest differences. When you look at your current staff, would being able to take an extra-long lunch break to work out because they are training for a triathlon be appreciated? Or being able to start at 10 a.m. so they can drop their kids off at school, or leave at 4 p.m. so they can pick their kids up, or go to school plays or do whatever else is important to them outside their work?

Autonomy over Time

Allowing your staff to have flexible working hours is giving them autonomy over their time. And of course there are ways to structure that so it's not a free-for-all. Globally there are lots of companies today that will say, "As long as you get your projects done on time, we don't care when you come in or when you leave."

Many other companies are moving towards a model that is strictly driven by Key Performance Indicators: "If you meet your KPIs and you're available for your clients, we don't care when you work, where you work, etc." (This, of course reinforces the importance of the Objectives Conversation.)

There also are companies that are doing away with annual leave and sick time: "You get your KPIs done and we don't care if you do it in 6 months or a year. You'll get paid for 12 months as long as you get your KPIs done." This is certainly the direction in which the workforce is heading.

Defining the Choice Continuum

Like our Motivators Continuum earlier in this chapter, there's a Choice Continuum too. You might consider offering your staff non-negotiable core hours and then flexibility around the beginning or ending of their day. For example, a company that offered greater choice might say, "Flexible working hours can be defined around core business hours of 10 a.m. and 4 p.m. Employees need to be at their desks (other than lunch break) between 10 a.m. and 4 p.m. But other than that, if you want to come in at 7:30 a.m. and leave at 4 p.m., that's fine. If you want to come in at 10 a.m. and leave at 6 p.m. or 7 p.m., that's fine."

But that doesn't mean managers are absolutely obliged to go this route. Maybe you run a team or an activity that simply cannot work like this. If so, you can say, "You know what? We've got to be here — we're not quite ready to go to flexible work hours." However, you may well have other forms of autonomy to offer to your employees that will positively align with their underlying motivators.

Flexibility and autonomy over time could be as simple as helping people understand when they are most productive and helping them to restructure their workday. It doesn't mean changing when they start or when they stop but simply changing the way they work, so they're working on certain types of tasks in the morning or at night.

A Choice Continuum Case Study

Yogesh's group was growing so rapidly that none of them had time to breathe. They were all working very long hours trying to get the projects out the door to satisfy customer demand. They knew this was a temporary but not short-term situation because it would take at least six weeks to hire the new staff they needed to meet their new workload.

Everyone was tired and some of the team were starting to get cranky and lose motivation. During one of his monthly conversations with a key staff member, Jane, Yogesh realized that she was feeling frustrated that she had no control over her time anymore. She was at work before the sun came up and there long after it went down. Even though she knew this was a temporary situation, she felt helpless, which made her angry.

Yogesh asked what Jane needed to feel more in control. He suspected that her answer might be something he couldn't deliver, given the current constraints. But much to his surprise she simply replied, "I want to leave at 3 p.m. Tuesday and Thursday to do an hour-long yoga class. I'll happily come back afterwards, but I need to know that I can have those two hours during the week, regardless of what is going on at work."

Yogesh quickly agreed. And with that flexibility implemented, Jane's attitude completely turned around. In fact, she became even more productive. He identified additional opportunities for his staff to regain some of their autonomy.

The workload didn't ease and it took three months instead of six weeks to find the additional staff they needed, but the team's motivation stayed high and they made it through without incident — and without anyone leaving the company.

Autonomy over Teams

Autonomy over teams can be the most difficult to implement owing to the variety of jobs people do. Often it is the client who selects the teams that will be working together — whether they are a "fit" or not. We've all seen what can happen on any team: some people get on really well together; in other instances, they have an instant dislike for each other. If they are all put on the same team, it doesn't necessarily mean that they will all be one big happy family.

However, autonomy around teams can be introduced when there are opportunities for cross-functional, non-work-related teams that you want to form. There may be a social event that needs arranging, a fun run that the company is putting a team together for, or a charity fundraiser that needs sponsors or prizes. Giving people the opportunity to play with people that they want to play with is a form of autonomy.

Within the working environment, you could consult with the potential people whose workloads would allow them to work on a specific project, and see who wants to play on that team and who doesn't. Sitting down, talking to them and giving them the choice within the business parameters — that's where the real juice within this lies. In this case, it's not even about the end result. It's about giving them the choice and helping them feel like they're controlling their own destiny.

Giving Choice Does Not Mean Rewarding Equally

Giving each member of a team more choice is not the same as dogmatically treating them all equally. Remember from our discussion on the three flavors of employees, *you don't need to, nor should you, treat your staff equally.* We *should* be playing favorites. We should be rewarding those who are performing the best, because that will encourage good behavior and good performance.

Autonomy over Tasks

Google famously encourages their staff to take 20 percent of the time or one day a week to work on whatever they want to work on. This could be a new product, a social justice cause or another special project. For every standard workweek, employees can take a full day to work on a project unrelated to their normal workload. Google claims that many of the products in Google Labs started out as pet projects in the 20 percent time program.

Hunter Walk heads up YouTube and has championed a project called "YouTube for Good." He has convinced about a fifth of YouTube's 1,000 or so employees, as well as others from Google's (YouTube's parent company) headquarters in Mountain View, California, to set aside a chunk of their time to build online tools used by organizations including the United Nations World Food Program and Charity: Water.

Walk promoted his effort as a way to make YouTube a place to learn about serious topics, not just a venue to watch music videos and cat videos. "There is a real desire for YouTube to be a global classroom and a global town square, not just global living room," Walk said in an interview with Bloomberg News. "I just needed to make a compelling, enthusiastic pitch."[30]

Autonomy of task can be called the *What and How Model.* For example, say you have three projects. You bring in your employee and say, "What do you want to work on?" When they make a choice, you respond, "Okay, this is *What* you're working on. I hired you because you've got the competencies and skills that I believe will enable you to do the job and be successful according to these KPIs. *How* you achieve these KPIs is up to you."

Google's "20 percent initiative" might not be possible for every organization. However, this autonomy over tasks allows staff to complete tasks to the best of their ability using their initiative.

Interestingly, the original "X percent initiative" was actually started by 3M — the inventors of sticky Post-It® notes, amongst other products. 3M stands for Minnesota Mining and Manufacturing. The company has been offering "15 percent time" since 1948 — a great example of an organization with an Industrial Age background that understood choice and motivators decades before so many others.[31] So it's not a new concept. Google just made it famous.

#2: Mastery

Mastery is the next dimension in Daniel Pink's AMP model. Desire for mastery of a technique, a task, a sport, or an art is an itch that most people cannot help scratching. *Kaizen,* the Japanese approach to continual improvement, is similar. You keep incrementally working away at something to get more and more insights into how to be better at it. Little by little, you achieve measurably more success.

There is a fundamentally important point about mastery in the AMP model. Whereas *kaizen* may be externally driven ("the company says do it this way"), the desire for mastery exists inside every person. That innate desire is stronger when the thing to be mastered matters more to you. It can also be stronger or weaker, according to whether or not you believe in your ability to improve at it.

As a manager, your role is to help your employees build a sufficiently solid base of belief that they can satisfy that itch to do better. It's also to be supportive of their efforts, because mastery will necessarily involve working both harder and longer at what they want to master. And when the improvement starts to show, you'll need to be on hand to help in a third way. As Pink points out, mastery is an *asymptote* — meaning, you can keep getting closer and closer without ever actually arriving. So help employees understand that while perfection may be unattainable, striving for excellence in their current role is truly a worthy cause.

Their striving for mastery will also form the basis for their professional development. What skills, abilities and experience do they need to attain to develop mastery? Fold these into training programs or action plans for the employee.

#3: Purpose

As the third factor in the AMP model, purpose binds together autonomy and mastery. Remember what we said about the Objectives Conversation and the need for employees to do work that is meaningful for them. When the purpose of the process is meaningful, autonomy and choice motivators will lubricate the process and the desire for mastery will accelerate it.

Which is a more important motivator: purpose or profit? Pink says: "Profit-driven approaches relegate purpose to a nice accessory if you want it, so long as it does not get in the way of the important stuff." He's right. Being permanently and myopically focused on profit excludes possibilities for staff to choose to go the extra mile. Ultimately, a purely profit-driven approach will be its own downfall.

Nevertheless, if you're struggling to remain afloat financially this quarter, then right now extra profit may mean the difference between swimming or sinking. That's the challenge for good managers. You are fated to look after both the short term and the long term. Use the tools in this book to help you do both in the most appropriate way possible.

How to Hold the Underlying Motivators Conversation

If you're like most modern managers (at least the ones who really care about motivating and managing staff not only for your benefit but theirs) you have probably intuited a lot of what we discussed above — but you just didn't know how to demystify what your staff thought and felt, or what they needed to be motivated to do their best work and go the extra mile. Hopefully, this background has given you a much better understanding. Now the only thing left to do is to have the actual conversation.

Preparing for the Conversation

As we have seen, the Locus of Motivation is a potent Underlying Motivator. An employee who can share his or her motivations through the Locus of Motivation tool is an employee who can be better rewarded according to preferences for internal challenges or external praise.

It is possible that members of your staff will not recognize their own Locus of Motivation, or will be unwilling to examine what they think really motivates them. They may also try to tell you what they think you want to hear as their manager: for example, that they are competitive with others, rather than being quietly focused on doing a good job.

For these reasons, assessing the Locus of Motivation needs to be done in two parts:

1. Have the Underlying Motivators Conversation with your staff. You can use Ignite Global's tool (http://igniteglobal.com/mrfm-book/), or simply craft questions similar to the earlier example.

2. Then observe how they act and react in the workplace to either confirm what you heard in the conversation, or investigate further.

As far as using the AMP model, there is really nothing to do to pre-pare for this conversation. This conversation simply consists of a dialogue between yourself and your individual staff members, designed to uncover what their drivers are in the areas of Autonomy, Mastery and Purpose and how you can help them achieve their needs in each of these areas.

As always, here are a few Conversation Starters you can use to get the ball rolling.

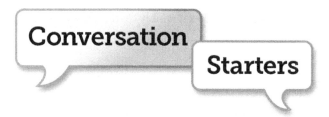

Use the Conversation Starters below to help your employees gain more au-tonomy, master their current job and feel that what they do professionally matters.

Autonomy Conversation Starters

- *Are you allowed to do what you need to do the best way you know how? If not, what do you need to do this?*

- *Is there anything you'd like to work on within the company that is not in your job description?*

- *Do you feel you have enough autonomy in your role? If not, what do you need to have more?*

- *How can I help you succeed? Do you need more or less of my time?*

- *If you were to redesign your role, what would you do differently and why?*

- *Do you have enough flexibility in your work hours?*

- *Do you feel like you have work/life balance? If not, what do you need to achieve that?*

- *Is there anyone on the team that you'd like to work with? If so, who and why? How could you do this?*

Mastery Conversation Starters

- *What do you need to become even better at your role than you are now? More training? What type? More resources? More time from a mentor (formal or informal)?*

- *What would you like to learn over the next 12 months to perform at a higher level?*

Purpose Conversation Starters

- *What attracted you to this profession/company/industry?*

- *When do you feel like you're doing your best work?*

- *When do you feel like you are contributing the most to customers, staff, your peers or others?*

Remember, we've been limiting employee potential because we haven't updated our approach to motivation as the work context has changed. Classic insights into motivation at work from Maslow and Herzberg among others help us better understand how motivators work. Use those in conjunction with other tools you've learned previously alongside the Locus of Motivation and the AMP models to boost your staff's sense of empowerment and to uncover and help them realize their individual drivers.

As a result, you will have more self-actualized employees who begin to lead rather than follow. They will become more creative, innovative and solutions oriented because they have "permission" to do so and the environment in which they work supports it.

And that's bound to make your job more interesting, less stressful, and perhaps even more fun!

Putting It into Action:
First Steps from This Chapter

Here are some tips for implementing the Underlying Motivators Conversation.

1. Consider each of your staff's Locus of Motivation. Where do they fall on the continuum? Do they respond more to internal motivation or external praise?

2. Introduce the Underlying Motivators Conversation with the Conversation Starters above.

3. Download the Motivators Continuum tool and ask them to complete it. Or design some questions for them to test your theories, based on the earlier example, and incorporate these questions into your monthly conversation.

4. Observe how they react to different motivators or methods of praise.

5. Choose one part of the AMP framework and incorporate it into the Unverlying Motivators Conversation.

8 | *FOCUSed* Conversation #5:

The Strengths Conversation

The Strengths Conversation at a Glance

1. Help your staff realize not only what they are good at but also what activities make them feel good.
2. Enable them to find ways to spend more time on those activities.
3. Assist them to find ways to manage or mitigate their weaknesses.

Why It's Important

Just as no one starts a job saying, "I really want to suck at this," very few will stay in a job where they are continuously asked to do things that they are bad at (or that make them feel bad). As we saw in our Currencies of Choice model, *people want to be able to do their best work every day.*

While this may seem obvious, being consistently asked to do things that we don't do well or that we hate is often part of our work culture.

Think about it. Weren't you taught as a child that, "To be successful we must learn to overcome our weaknesses" or that you must become a "well-rounded" individual?

But when you came home from school with a report card that read:

- English: A
- Science: A
- Math: B
- History: C

Which grades got the most attention from your parents? Which grade gets the most attention from you now, as a parent? The A's? The B? Probably not. Your parents probably focused in on the C and had a discussion about how you could bring that up.

This is the culture that we live in. These are the rules that we've lived by for centuries.

But a growing mountain of evidence says that they are wrong.

The Growth of a Movement

The Strengths Movement has been around at least since the time of management guru Peter Drucker, who said in 1992, "A manager's task is to make the strengths of people effective and their weakness irrelevant."[32]

But the Gallup Organization is probably best known for their work in this area. They have published several books on strengths, discussing the results from their incredible body of research spanning more than 30 years and including interviews with more than two million individuals and tens of thousands of work teams.[33]

Remember our statistics from Chapter 2? Teams that play to their strengths experience:

- 37 percent lower absenteeism
- Up to 65 percent lower employee turnover

- 48 percent fewer safety incidents
- 41 percent fewer quality incidents (defects)
- 10 percent higher customer metrics
- 21 percent higher productivity
- 22 percent higher profitability

So, focusing on strengths is *good for the bottom line.*

Now, if you've already made the leap to the fact that focusing on strengths is also good for employee engagement, you'd be right. In their book, *Strengths Based Leadership*, Tom Rath and Barry Conchie state:

> *In the workplace, when an organization's leadership fails to focus on individuals' strengths, the odds of an employee being engaged are a dismal 1 in 11 (9 percent). But when an organization's leadership focuses on the strengths of its employees, the odds soar to almost 3 in 4 (73 percent). When leaders focus on and invest in their employees' strengths, the odds of each person being engaged goes up eightfold.*[34]

"But wait," you might be saying. "How does this gel with what I've been taught all my life about how I have to shore up my weaknesses to grow the most and to be successful?"

It doesn't — and that's the point.

The research is clearly showing that *we grow the most in the areas of our strengths.* The seminal study that demonstrated this fact was conducted by the University of Nebraska back in 1955, when over 1,000 students were tested for reading speed.

The slow readers' pre-test showed an average reading speed of 90 words per minute, while the fast readers' average speed was clocked at 350 words per minute. Both groups took the same speed reading course and were tested again.

The slow readers increased their speed from 90 words to 150 words per minute — a 66 percent increase! Impressive, right?

And the fast readers? Traditional wisdom would say that the fast readers would not improve as *much* as the slow readers, right? Traditional thinking tells us that the worse we are at something, the more room we have to grow.

But that's not what the evidence says. The fast readers' average post-test score was an incredible *2,900 words per minute!* They increased by an average of *825 percent.*[35]

So, playing to your strengths is not only good for business and good for employee engagement (and thus you as a manager). It's also good for you, and your staff, as an individual.

Take for instance the research conducted by CAPP, a strengths-based testing and consulting firm based in the U.K. It shows that people who play to their strengths more:

- Are happier
- Are more confident
- Have higher levels of self-esteem
- Have higher levels of energy and vitality
- Experience less stress
- Are more resilient
- Are more likely to achieve their goals
- Perform better at work
- Are more engaged at work
- Are more effective at developing themselves and growing as individuals[36]

It's time to make the paradigm shift. Focusing on strengths is a Social Age concept and one that is gaining speed.

How much time and energy have we all spent stressing out about having to become better at activities or tasks that we are just not good at? Wouldn't it be wonderful to let ourselves off the hook and to instead concentrate on learning to utilize our innate talents better and more often? To spend our time on activities that make us feel energetic, confident, powerful, optimistic and joyful rather than those that regularly leave us feeling angry, frustrated, annoyed, depleted, depressed or confused?

Of course it would. And how much better would our conversations feel with staff if we concentrated on what they were doing well instead of where they were lacking?

Impossible? As we've seen the research tells us otherwise. So let's take a leap of faith and explore this a little further.

It's time to change the way we define a strength.

What Is the Strengths Conversation?

Traditionally a strength was considered something that you are good at. But that's only partially true. Both Marcus Buckingham, who was involved in the original Gallup research, and CAPP, which has done extensive research on its own, say that the traditional definition lacks energy: specifically *positive energy and emotion*. This is where the strengths movement intersects with the work done in the field of behavioral psychology (more on that in a minute).

But first, let's look at a very interesting model by CAPP, the 4M Model, which explains this concept of energy in more detail.[37]

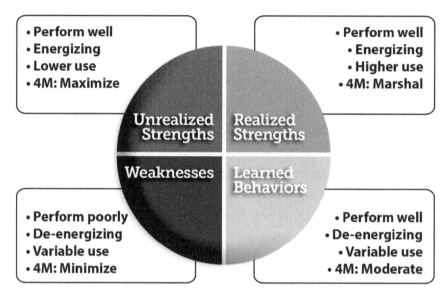

- **Perform well**
- **Energizing**
- **Lower use**
- **4M: Maximize**

- **Perform well**
- **Energizing**
- **Higher use**
- **4M: Marshal**

Unrealized Strengths

Realized Strengths

Weaknesses

Learned Behaviors

- **Perform poorly**
- **De-energizing**
- **Variable use**
- **4M: Minimize**

- **Perform well**
- **De-energizing**
- **Variable use**
- **4M: Moderate**

CAPP states that this model "represents the core theory and research on which Realise2 [their profiling tool] is based, representing the four combinations of energy, performance, and use, which together define the four quadrants of the model."

While profiling tools are useful, they can only tell you what your strengths are in broad terms. So, for example, if you were to use Gallup's profiling tool, *Strengths Finder 2.0,* you might find out that one of your top five strengths themes is Achiever. Gallup defines this theme, in part, as:

> *Your Achiever helps explain your drive. Achiever describes a constant need for achievement. You feel as if every day starts at zero. By the end of the day you must achieve something tangible in order to feel good about yourself.*[38]

Great information to be sure, but how does this relate to those activities that you do every day? Sometimes the connection is obvious; other times it's not so straightforward.

In order to be really useful and practical, we need to look at the activities that we do on a daily basis and figure out if they play to our strengths or not. Once we determine that, we can then make decisions about which activities:

- we should spend more time/less time doing, or
- we should invest the most time and resources in learning to do better.

We can also start to think about how to manage or mitigate our weaknesses, because we will never ever have a job (or manage an employee) where all our time is spent strictly on activities that play to our strengths.

So, let's look at this model slightly differently. Instead of *energy, performance* and *use,* let's think in terms of *capability, energy* and *capacity.*

Stated differently, the 4M Model combines your *capability* (whether you are naturally good at these activities) with your *energy* (whether you feel positively or negatively about doing them) with your *capacity* (how often you do them in your daily work life). This is a subtle but important difference.

Starting with the top right quadrant, CAPP defines a **realized strength** as one that is characterized by high energy, high performance, and high use. This means that:

- you *feel positively* about doing these activities,
- you *are good* at them, and
- you do them often.

A **learned behavior** is characterized by lower energy but high performance, while use may be variable. This means that:

- you *feel negatively* about doing these activities, but
- you *are good* at them, and
- you may or may not do them often.

A **weakness** is characterized by lower energy and lower performance, while again use may be variable. This means that:

- you *feel negatively* about doing these activities, and
- you *are not good* at them, and
- you may or may not do them often.

And finally, an **unrealized strength** is characterized by high energy and high performance, but lower use. This means that:

- you *feel positively* about doing these activities, and
- you *are good* at them, but
- you do not do them often.

These four characteristics — realized strengths, learned behaviors, weaknesses and unrealized strengths — together make up the four quadrants of the Realise2 4M Model.

The "4M's" refer to the advice that comes from the model, following clockwise:

- *Marshal* realized strengths: use them appropriately for your situation and context
- *Moderate* learned behaviors: use them in moderation and only when you need to
- *Minimize* weaknesses: use them as little as possible and only where necessary
- *Maximize* unrealized strengths: find opportunities to use them more

We will discuss how to apply this model to our own day-to-day activities a bit later. Let's now dissect each of the three components of the model: capability, energy and capacity.

Capability: What You Are Good at and Why

The capability component speaks directly to how good you are at this particular type of activity. This goes back to the original definition of the word strength as *something you are good at.*

But have you ever stopped to ask yourself *why* you are good at these particular things? It can't *just* be a matter of training and repetition, can it? Remember the reading test? If this were the case, that would mean that everyone who went through the same type of training for the same duration would experience the same increase, right? But that clearly didn't happen. Nor does that happen in real life. You are *naturally* better at some things than others. You are *naturally* worse at some things than others. Why?

To answer this, we need to turn to the fields of behavioral psychology and neuroscience. (A word of warning… this is a very rudimentary explanation of a very complex topic, and more research is being done every day in these two areas.)

The Complete Idiot's Guide to Neuroscience

The fields of behavioral psychology and neuroscience have discovered that our innate abilities — those that we are *naturally* good at — are neurologically hardwired into our brains between the ages of 3 and 15. It works something like this…

From the minute we are born (and possibly before) we are bombarded by stimuli from all of our senses. To make sense of these stimuli and to store information, memories and behavior, our brains form neural pathways.

Billions of these pathways are formed between the time we are born and about the age of three. Some of these pathways are used over and over and over again (if I cry I will get picked up and held or fed). Others are not used very frequently at all.

Between ages 3 and 15 the pathways that are not frequently used die off or become much weaker. But those that are used again and again and again become stronger.

A good analogy might be to imagine hiking through an open field. If this were the first time you came across this field you would see no clear path. Similar to behavior, there is no clear way to act. However, once you find a way through, you might come back the next day to see that your tracks were faintly visible and you could probably retrace your steps. If you were to hike in this field every day for the next 30 days, by the end of the month there would be a clear path trodden into the dirt. That particular way would be the path of least resistance and you would continue to follow it.

The brain works very similarly. If you exhibit the same behaviors time after time, the way your neurons fire is similar to the path being trodden down in the field by your repeatedly walking through it. The repeated behavior becomes a natural reaction. Then if something happens which triggers that reaction, you will behave a certain way because that's how your neurons have "learned" to fire.

For instance, let's say you are five years old and are sitting in a sandbox with Jane and Bob, two kids from the neighborhood. It's just after Christmas and they both have two new sets of toys. But you didn't bring yours out that day. You might ask Jane if you can borrow her toys or play with her.

Now, let's say that Jane has many brothers and sisters at home and always has to share. Let's also imagine that none of her siblings are around on this particular day and she decides to assert her independence for the first time in her young life and she says "No." You might then ask John the same question and he may agree.

If Jane feels good about asserting her independence she may find herself doing so again and again. Her neural pathways become stronger and stronger, and playing (or working) alone may become her natural behavior.

If John feels good about sharing and collaborating with you, he might actually seek out activities where he can do that more and more.

The context of the behavior changes, but the behaviors do not. New research on neuroplasticity (the brain's ability to change neural pathways and to grow new neurons throughout your lifetime) notwithstanding, scientists believe that once you reach the age of 15 your behaviors, innate abilities and talents are fairly well set for life.

This means that John will grow up to become a more collaborative person in the workplace than Jane. That doesn't mean that Jane can't become *more* collaborative. With coaching and training, she can become better at sharing her metaphorical "toys" on the job. But in the context of the strengths research, she will never become as good at being collaborative as John. Remember, the slow readers scores improved, but not nearly as significantly as the fast readers.

So, how does this relate to activities on the job? The natural behaviors or competencies that became "hardwired" in your brain between 3 and 15 underpin those activities that you are good at and those that you are not so good at. In other words, your strengths are the reasons you excel at some of your duties and responsibilities and not others.

Again, you could approach discovering your strengths in this way. You could do a strengths profile and then look for activities that match those strengths from your profile. And that's useful, but again, it may not be obvious or practical.

Let's take a look at how we can accomplish this in a more practical manner by flipping it around and looking at what we do that makes us *feel good* first and then figuring out if we are also good at those activities. Which brings us to the second component of the 4M Model, Energy.

Energy: What Makes You Feel Good

Is there a task or piece of work that you *hate* to do but that always ends up on your desk? Do people consistently ask you to take on projects you dislike because you're so good at them? That's pretty common. For instance, you might be someone who is not naturally good at detail, but over the course of your career you had to become good at doing things like writing very de-

© iStock/RapidEye

tailed documents and plans. Perhaps you started a business early in your career and you had to write winning proposals with very detailed project plans in order to eat. So you became good at them, but they drain you.

However, because you are so good at them, you keep getting tasks that require very detailed project plans dropped on your desk.

In the context of the 4M Model above, these are considered *Learned Behaviors*. Because these are learned, and not innate or natural, no matter how often you do them you will never feel good about them.

This is where the concept of energy comes in. Think back to the sandbox scenario. It's possible that the very reason John became good at collaborating is because the first time he did so he felt good about his behaviors. So he looked for additional opportunities to be collaborative until, by age 15, it was natural or innate. Maybe the neural connections followed the emotions.

This is the premise we are going to use here. How you feel about an activity gives you clues about those activities that you are *naturally* good at (or can become good at) and those that truly are weaknesses.

But energy plays another important role in strengths as they relate to employee engagement. Will your staff be engaged if they are repeatedly asked to do something that makes them feel bad? No, of course they won't.

A Learned Behavior Strengths Conversation Case Study

I was in the midst of teaching a Strengths workshop to a group of managers when I looked up to see the face of Matt (one of the participants) turning white. He was visibly shaken.

When I questioned him about it Matt replied, "I can't believe it! I have an employee in our Western Suburbs office — let's call him 'John' — who's really good at doing a particular type of project. And increasingly when I've given him these projects, he's kicked up a fuss about them.

"Recently he's been joking about it, saying, 'You keep giving me this work to do and I'm going to have to find another job!' At least I thought it was a joke — now I realize that he might be serious.

"I thought he was joking because he's so good at it. I thought to myself, 'How can you hate something that you're so good at?' Now after doing this workshop I realize that it is not tongue-in-cheek. Even though he is fantastic at that task, he really hates doing it."

I then asked Matt what he was going to do about the situation now that it had been identified.

He said, "Tomorrow I am going out to see John and have a conversation with him."

And he did. Matt took some of the Strengths Conversation Starters, asked John about his strengths, and really engaged him in conversation, as follows:

Matt: So what you are telling me is this particular project that I keep asking you to do, you really hate doing this. You don't feel that this is an area of your strength, because this does not make you feel strong?

John: Absolutely. I hate doing this kind of work.

Matt: Okay, what if I told you that I really understand this now, and we will have to find someone else in the office who can be trained to pick it up. Would you be willing to help out?

John: Not only would I be willing to help out and to train whomever takes this over, I can promise you that I'll stop seeing recruiters now.

John was, in fact, looking for another job. But that conversation (and the actions that followed it) allowed him to stay. This happened more than two years ago and as of this writing John is still a valuable and productive employee — who is no longer asked to do that type of project work.

In order to use these feelings as an indicator though, we need to think about patterns. Everyone has a bad day when you just don't feel good. Everyone gets busy and overwhelmed from time to time. Then you may have negative feelings even about activities or tasks that normally make you feel great.

When you think about the activities that you do in the course of your normal workday, week or month, think about how these activities regularly and consistently make you feel.

It's Not Kumbaya

Don't mistake *good feelings* for holding hands and singing Kumbaya. The feelings you want to look for (and help your staff to look for) are any positive emotions, but particularly those that make you *feel strong*. It makes sense, doesn't it? A strength is what makes you feel strong. Here are two lists of words that you can look for when gauging whether your activities make you feel strong — or the opposite.

Which activities regularly make you feel strong or weak?

Strengths Indicators: Strong, powerful, confident, I've got this, on top of the world, alive, in the zone, joyful, light, easy to do, happy, blissful, satisfied, optimistic, hopeful

Weakness Indicators: Weak, depleted, depressed, angry, frustrated, miffed, annoyed, tired, avoidance, sad, resigned, can't wait for it to be over, no way out

---

Note the words that are *not* in the box: fearful, terrified, apprehensive…. You may actually feel these feelings when you are thinking about an *unrealized strength* — something that you have the capability to be naturally good at but may not have developed your desired competence in yet. We will talk about this a bit later.

Exercise: Identify Your Own Strengths

© iStock/pavlen

Before you begin to work with your staff on their strengths, take a moment to look at yours.

- Take a piece of paper and draw a vertical line down the center.
- On the left, write down activities, tasks, responsibilities, etc., that you do in the normal course of your work that consistently make you feel good.

- On the right, write a list of those activities, tasks, responsibilities, etc., that consistently make you feel bad.

If doing this exercise makes you feel like a deer in headlights ("I can't think of anything!") then try an exercise from the Ignite Global workshops. This was adapted from an exercise originally proposed by psychology professor Mihaly Csikszentmihalyi, who is credited with originating the concept of flow. Flow, as he describes it, is when you are "in the zone" and time just disappears because you are fully engaged and immersed in your work. We are not strictly looking for those activities that put you in the state of *flow*, but this exercise can be very helpful to determine how you feel about what you do.

Exercise: Come Flow with Me

On Sunday night (or whatever night precedes the start of your work week), set alarms on your phone (if you don't have a smartphone, borrow one).

Aim to set between 20 to 50 alarms (depending on how quickly you change tasks) at random times throughout the workday. When each alarm goes off, immediately check in. What are you feeling? Write down what you are doing and how it is making you feel. You can use the above-mentioned paper divided down the center or you can simply keep a running list — whichever is easier.

Note: It's important to *first* recognize your feelings and *then* what you are doing. Why? Because thinking about what you are doing may cloud your feelings about it. For instance, you might be making a specific type of sales call that consistently makes you feel annoyed. But your job is sales! You can't not like something that's such an integral part of your job, so you might find yourself justifying and not writing down your true feelings.

But you can (and probably do) not like things that are integral to your work, and we will talk about how to deal with that later.

When Energy Meets Capability, It Spawns Capacity

Okay, so now it's time to marry the three concepts of Capability, Energy and Capacity. Look at your list of regular work activities categorized by positive and negative feelings. First, look at those activities in your strengths column and further divide them into two categories: those you currently feel competent in (i.e. you're good at them) and those that you are not as competent as you would like.

Those tasks that make you feel good and that you are currently quite competent in are your *realized strengths,* according to the 4M Model above. You should look for more opportunities to do these types of activities.

Those tasks that make you feel good, but that you feel you could become better at to reach the level of competency you desire, are your *unrealized strengths.* You should look for both ways to up-skill in these areas as well as opportunities to do them more (which will help you up-skill as well).

Now let's look at those activities in your weaknesses column. Again, rate your competency for each of these.

As we've talked about before, those activities that invoke negative feelings but that you are good at are your *learned behaviors.* Those where both your capability and energy are poor (i.e. those that you both hate and suck at) are your true *weaknesses.* Regardless of whether something is a learned behavior or a real weakness, you should look at ways of limiting any activities in this column.

A strength is….

- An innate ability or behavioral pattern
- Hardwired into our brain between ages 3-15
- Remains a consistent pattern through life

Your strengths underpin those activities that make you feel good

How do you recognize a strength?

- An activity that *regularly* makes you feel good and
- That you are good at *or* can become good at

Shifting Responsibilities

Now let's look at how to incorporate more of those activities that play to your strengths and less of those that you would classify as a weakness into your workday.

When I say that, most people protest, "How do I do that? I live in the real world where I can't pick and choose what I do!"

It's true: as we've said before, you will never have a job (nor manage staff) where all activities play to your (or their) strengths. But according to studies of strengths usage, freeing up just two hours per week from activities that make you feel weak and replacing them with those that make you feel strong can make an exponential difference in your overall effectiveness, your enjoyment and your (or your staff's) engagement levels.

There are three ways to manage or mitigate your weaknesses or learned behaviors:

- Stop doing them (with or without permission)
- Delegate, trade or collaborate
- Figure out how to make doing them more palatable

#1: Just Stop (and See If Anyone Notices)

Have you ever found yourself in a regularly scheduled meeting that you feel has long outlived its usefulness? Or creating a report you suspect no one reads? Or answering an email where you *know* your opinion won't hold any sway?

In the modern corporate world, we are great at starting new initiatives and fairly poor at re-evaluating them from time to time to make sure that they are still applicable and relevant.

One of the easiest ways to free up two hours per week is to look at the activities in your weaknesses column and to ask yourself if you can just stop doing any of them. You may or may not have to get someone's buy-in to do this. But the old expression may hold true here, "It's easier to ask forgiveness than permission."

#2: Delegate, Trade or Collaborate

For those activities that you can't just stop, ask yourself if there is anyone on your team to whom you can "empower with additional responsibility" (i.e. delegate).

If you can't delegate, then you can look for someone else for whom this is actually a strength. One man's trash (or weakness) is another man's treasure (or strength). Either work with them (collaborate) or trade with them (find something in their weaknesses column that appears in your strengths).

#3: Suck It Up and Try to Make It More Palatable

Finally, if you can't just stop doing this activity and there is no one to delegate to or collaborate or trade with, then you might just have to suck it up. We do live in the real world and there will always be tasks that we do regularly that fall into the learned behavior or weakness quadrants.

So how do we make this more palatable? Here are some ideas to make your learned behavior or weaknesses more palatable:

- **Do them during the time of day where you naturally feel the strongest.** Are you a morning person, or do you only come alive after your third cup of coffee, or lunch? Whatever time of day you feel at your most energetic is the time of day to attack those activities that make you feel weak, because you have a natural reserve of energy to get you through.

- **Make a game out of it, or think about it in terms of one of your strengths.** Are you competitive (or motivated by internal challenge from the chapter on the Underlying Motivators Conversation)? If so, you could set up a competition with yourself. Beat your last time, or get just a bit better result than the one you got before.

- **Reward yourself.** Give yourself a prize (allow yourself ten minutes to check Facebook during the day, go for a walk around the block, buy yourself an extra large latte, play the full 18 holes of golf on Saturday instead of your regular 9). Come up with something to motivate you to do this activity as fast and as competently as you can.

A Delegate, Trade or Collaborate Case Study

Kumar and Renata both worked as recruiters who placed temporary and contract professional staff. Not being detail-oriented, Kumar hated to fill out expense reports, but fill them out he must — weekly if he wanted to get paid. But Renata loved doing them. She loved the fact that it was one of the few tasks that was black and white in the sea of her other activities that seemed to be colored in various shades of grey.

Kumar thought Renata was crazy, but he took her to lunch one day with a proposal. If she filled in his expense reports he would do the thing she hated most. He would stay back two hours once a week to make candidate update calls. Every recruiter on a temp desk was required to make calls to his or her available candidates once a week to make sure that they were still available and to gather market information from them. Since Kumar was required to do this for his own candidates, this would require him to stay back an additional two hours on a different night than he did his own.

Renata thought this job was boring and a little invasive, having to ask about the candidate's other interviews and other market information.

Kumar loved doing these calls. He loved the thrill of the chase. If he could find out where the candidates were interviewing, perhaps he could call those prospective clients the next day and bring in more jobs to fill.

Kumar was willing, even enthusiastic about trading expense reports for candidate update calls, even though it would require more time and effort on his part.

Renata was keen as well. So they traded and the system worked flawlessly — until Renata moved on to another branch. Kumar couldn't find someone else to trade tasks with after Renata had left, but he did find someone who was willing to do his expense reports in return for a nice, expensive lunch out — another sacrifice Kumar was happily willing to make!

A Make It More Palatable Case Study

Carlo worked at the front desk of a beautiful old hotel in downtown Nashville, Tennessee. He loved working the front desk because he was a real people person. Being in Nashville, he got to meet fabulous people, some of them very famous. One of Carlo's personal victories was that Lionel Ritchie brought him coffee one morning to thank him for doing a great job.

The General Manager of the hotel saw a lot of potential in Carlo and wanted to give him more experience. He asked Carlo to work in the hotel's internal accounting department two days per week to give him a bit of general business experience as well as introducing him to some of the other department heads.

Carlo jumped at that opportunity and for the most part relished his new responsibilities. Except one: payroll. Even though the recently restored hotel was built in the early 1900s everything about it was modern — except for the payroll system. That was still very manual.

So Carlo had to come in every Saturday morning, collect the time cards from the old time clock area, add up the daily hours to calculate a weekly total, manually transfer the cards to the payroll register generated by the home office, multiply the total hours worked by the hourly rate appearing on the payroll register and add up the totals on each sheet to generate a grand total for both hours worked and wages to be paid.

It was tedious work and Carlo hated it. But he knew that he had to "pay his dues" and do some things that were boring and tedious in the short term to reach his long-term goals.

So he made a game of it. Carlo was very competitive. He

played sports and had been in the high school band just a year earlier. He was always at the top of the league tables and played first chair clarinet.

So Carlo began to keep track of how long it would take him to do each step of the payroll process. His goal every week was to beat his previous week's time. After a few weeks he actually began to have fun doing payroll. But that didn't stop him from celebrating when they finally installed a modern system.

How does someone add more strengths to their workday? Start small: look for ways to free up just a few minutes per day or per week. It will build over time. Once you do, look for ways to marshal your unrealized strengths and to maximize your realized strengths. And you can do the same with your staff.

How Do You Play to Strengths and Manage or Mitigate Weaknesses?

1. Identify them: understand both strengths and weaknesses.

2. Have a conversation with your manager and team about why playing to your strengths more will help the team and the organization.

3. Stop, delegate, collaborate or trade learned behaviors and weaknesses, or find ways of making them more palatable.

4. Identify ways to increase opportunities to play to your strengths.

How to Hold the Strengths Conversation

This brings us back to the actual conversation. There is no difference in holding this conversation with staff to what we've done together above. And there is really nothing to do to plan for this conversation, since the *only* person who can truly know what activities make them feel strong is each of your employees.

To have these conversations, simply:

- Begin with one of the Conversation Starters below
- Explain the concept of strengths and weaknesses, using the above definitions
- Help them identify their own strengths and weaknesses, if they need help — again, you can use the Conversation Starters
- Help them identify ways to manage or mitigate learned behaviors and weaknesses to free up a couple of hours per week
- Help them identify ways to incorporate more activities that are their realized strengths and to identify ways to become better at (and do more of) activities that fall into the unrealized strengths quadrant

Conversation Starters

- *I'd like to talk to you about your strengths and weaknesses. Normally when managers have conversations like this with staff we concentrate on weaknesses. I don't want to do this. I want to concentrate on your strengths. Let me share a few facts with you that might help you understand why (refer to statistics above).*

- *I want to spend some time talking about your strengths and how you can do more on a day-to-day basis that will allow you to play to them. But I want to use a different definition of the word strength. Let me explain (go through the above concepts).*

If they need help to determine their **strengths,** ask:

- *What makes you feel really strong and confident at work?*
- *Which of your tasks really lights you up or excites you?*
- *What do you look forward to doing each day/week/month?*
- *Which of your duties/responsibilities do you get lost in, where time just slips by?*
- *What part of your work are you most proud of?*
- *Which responsibilities make you feel the best when you complete them?*

If they need to determine their **learned behaviors** or **weaknesses,** ask:

- *What do you do regularly that makes you feel depleted, frustrated, angry or drained?*
- *What tasks do you find time just dragging on?*

After you have your Strengths Conversations with your staff, your involvement will be determined by the level of staff you manage. Once the concept is explained to them, the more senior staff will be perfectly capable of determining ways to free up their time by managing or mitigating their learned behaviors and weaknesses and incorporating more of what makes them feel strong on a daily basis. For the more junior staff, you may have to help them through this process a bit more. But it's important to give them the autonomy to do so on their own — especially at first.

Regardless of the level of person you are working with, remind them that one person's strength is another person's weakness, so they shouldn't be afraid of approaching someone to collaborate with or trade.

Many teams do this together. Once they understand the strengths concept, they will come together to have an activities auction. They trade duties and responsibilities in a fun way. The teams collaborate and figure out how to help everybody on the team work more to their strengths.

Once you have this conversation with your entire team and once everyone (including you) is spending more time playing to their strengths you will find that everyone enjoys their jobs more and you will reap the benefits that Gallup, CAPP and others have found in their research.

Putting It into Action: First Steps from This Chapter

Here are some tips for implementing the Strengths Conversation.

1. Use the Conversation Starters on pages 166–167 to introduce the topic.

2. Have/help them to categorize their activities into strengths and weaknesses.

3. Explain the 4M Quadrant and the difference between:
   - Realized strengths
   - Learned behaviors
   - Weaknesses
   - Unrealized strengths

4. Have/help them further categorize their activities into the four quadrants.

5. Have/help them design strategies to manage or mitigate learned behaviors and weaknesses.

6. Have/help them design strategies to play more to their strengths.

Notes

9 | The Mind Reading Manager's Secrets for Success

People want to know they matter and they want to be treated as people. That's the new talent contract.

Pamela Stroko, Talent Management Expert & Evangelist, Oracle Corporation

Remember the Currencies of Choice — those factors that must be met for employees to be fully engaged? People want to:

1. Work for someone they trust and respect in a company they can support

2. Work with people they like

3. Be appreciated

4. Have their voices and opinions respected

5. Understand how to be successful in their role

6. Have a career path (vertical or horizontal) that keeps them motivated and interested

7. Be inspired to go the extra mile and suitably recognized and rewarded appropriately when they do

8. Be able to do what they do best every day

Your staff members are far more motivated by *intrinsic* motivators than they are *extrinsic* ones — and the intrinsic motivators that make the most difference are the Currencies of Choice. Indeed, the 5 *FOCUSed* Conversations were designed to make sure that these eight points are addressed on a regular basis.

Let's summarize the 5 *FOCUSed* Conversations and the elements that go into each.

#1: The Feedback Conversation

- Share company news/updates.
- Give praise where praise is due.
- Give them a voice and allow them to share frustrations as well as ideas.

#2: The Objectives Conversation

- Set specific, measurable job objectives and get agreement about them with staff member. Make sure the job objectives are a description of *what*, not *how*, and provide clear criteria by which success will be measured. A robust job objective answers three questions: (1) What is the outcome to be achieved? (2) How will it be measured? (3) Does this align with a larger purpose or integrate into a community?
- Check in monthly for accountability. Are they on track to meet their goals/achieve their objectives? If not, why not? Do they need more time, training, resources? What other obstacles are in their way? Then manage the gap and course correct during the month.
- Review objectives quarterly and adjust for circumstantial changes.

#3: The Career Development Conversation

- Ensure your staff members' professional goals are aligned with and support their personal ones.

  — Make sure that their professional goals are truly their own and that they are positively motivated about achieving them for the right reasons.

- Determine what, if anything, about their job, their manager (you), their team or their work environment is frustrating them and how these frustrations can be fixed. Remember that sometimes the smallest things make the biggest difference.

- Help them build resilience to overcome setbacks.

#4: The Underlying Motivators Conversation

- Use the Locus of Motivation to determine whether staff members are motivated more by Internal Challenge or External Praise and where they fall on the Motivators Continuum between the two.

- Use Daniel Pink's framework to assess staff members' Underlying Motivators of *Autonomy, Mastery* and *Purpose.* Incorporate discussion of one of these motivators into this conversation.

#5: The Strengths Conversation

- Help your staff realize not only what they are good at but also what activities make them feel good.

- Use the CAPP 4M Model to assess *realized strengths, learned behaviors, weaknesses* and *unrealized strengths.* Discuss their *capability* (whether they are naturally good at these activities), *energy* (whether they feel positively or negatively about doing them) and *capacity* (how often they use these traits in daily work life).

- Help them to find ways to spend more time to *marshal* realized strengths by using them appropriately for the situation and context; and to *maximize* unrealized strengths by finding opportunities to use them more.

- Assist them to *moderate* learned behaviors — use them in moderation and only when needed — and to *minimize* weaknesses by using these skills as little as possible and only where necessary.

- They can manage or mitigate a weakness in three ways: (1) stop doing the activity, (2) delegate, trade or collaborate with someone who's good at or enjoys the activity, or (3) suck it up and figure out how to make doing it more palatable.

Throughout this book you've seen references to the tools you can download at http://igniteglobal.com/mrfmbook/. I really want to encourage you to take advantage of the tools provided, especially the **FOCUSed** Conversations Planning Calendar. It will help you keep your scheduling of the 5 **FOCUSed** Conversations straight with each of your employees.

But if you're not one for a structured program, you might want to consider something more simple by creating a meeting schedule that might look like:

MONTH 1: Feedback *only*

MONTH 2: Feedback and Objectives

MONTH 3: Feedback, Objectives, Career Development

MONTH 4: Feedback, Objectives, Underlying Motivators

MONTH 5: Feedback, Objectives, Strengths

In Month 6 you could elect to start the cycle again, or you and your staff member could choose the **FOCUSed** Conversation that you believe would have the most benefit. Sometimes the staff member will make the choice; sometimes the manager will have an issue in mind that requires a particular conversation. But *always remember to include time for feedback and reviewing objectives in every meeting.* This will ensure that the two-way communication between you and your staff stays strong.

Suggestions for Success

I have presented this program as a framework consisting of five distinct conversations — which they are, in theory. But in practice, communication is typically messy: rarely linear, mostly disjointed and layered with nuances, tangents and starts and stops. In reality, you will find that these conversations will bleed into each other from month to month. And that's okay. The goal is to create an ongoing dialogue between you and your staff that will allow you both to stay more fully engaged.

Now that you have an understanding behind the 5 *FOCUSed* Conversations, here are a few suggestions for success.

- You should schedule monthly conversations to talk about only these topics.

- These conversations should be separate and distinct from any operational issues or other meetings you have with staff.

- Have the first conversation with your staff telling them that you are committed to doing this. Get them excited about it by painting a vivid picture of how this will help them, the team and you. Get their buy-in and ask them to hold you accountable until it becomes habit.

- Schedule your first meetings with each staff member, and put time in your calendar to plan those first meetings.

- Get clear on the benefits of taking some time out to have these conversations. Visualize the benefits just like a top athlete visualizes success on the golf course or tennis court.

- Schedule subsequent meetings (and prep time) at the end of your first meeting with each staff member to keep the momentum rolling.

- Review job objectives quarterly with your staff and hold them accountable monthly.

- Break the Career Development, Underlying Motivators and Strengths Conversations into bite-sized chucks (use the *FOCUSed* Conversation Planner to help you) and cover each of these three to four times per year, depending on the staff member.

- Feel free to mix and match the 5 *FOCUSed* Conversations. The most important thing is that you have these talks with staff and you cover these five topics.

- Plan for the conversation as you would an extremely important meeting with your own manager — chances are your staff members can make as much of an impact through their performance as you would in reporting their results to your boss.

- Document the conversations so that you can keep track of them from month to month.

- Buy your team copies of this book and have them work the program with you. Hold each other accountable.

- Make it fun! Don't look at it as a chore. Look at it as an opportunity to get to know your staff better and to create a more healthy work environment.

- Don't beat yourself up if you slide back into old habits. It's normal. Just restart.

- Remember, Rome wasn't built in a day. It takes 4 to 8 months to really instill behavioral change in yourself and your staff. Schedule check-ins for yourself to make sure you stay on track.

How to Use These Conversations with Your Own Manager

In my *Mind Reading for Managers* workshops inevitably someone will come up to me during a break and ask quietly, "Is there a way I can use this with my manager?" My advice is to structure the program in reverse. Here's a simple three-step process.

#1: Speak to your manager the way they can understand and let them see how this might be of benefit.

The first step in proper communication is being able to talk to your manager in a way he or she can understand. Take a look at the Underlying Motivators Conversation and see if you can determine your manager's Locus of Motivation (Internal Challenge or External Praise) or their preferred Currencies of Choice. You can then use this to speak with your manager in his or her "language."

Remember, people have different personalities and communication styles, but everyone wants to know, "What's in it for me?" Put together a list of potential benefits to your department, your direct reports, your manager and the organization as a whole if you could utilize the 5 **FOCUSed** Conversations tool as a structure for your communication.

#2. Have an initial conversation telling your manager what you need to be successful and proposing a structured feedback session framework.

Schedule a meeting with your boss at a time when you know you'll have at least 15 uninterrupted minutes. Then have a conversation explaining that you need their help (very few people, especially managers, will refuse someone a genuine request for help).

Tell your boss that you would like to meet regularly to discuss a few things that will be helpful for your productivity and effectiveness in the job as well as your own career development and job satisfaction. Let him or her know that you're really interested in doing the best job you can in your role and continuing to learn, grow and develop in this position and with this company.

Say that you would like 30 minutes to an hour of their time every month for one of the 5 *FOCUSed* Conversations. (Feel free to share this book to give them an idea of what you wish to cover.) You also can let them know that you'll be driving these conversations so it shouldn't be an added burden on them, and you will send them an agenda before each conversation to let them know what you wish to discuss.

In particular, you might want to emphasize the following points for each conversation.

The Feedback Conversation: Let them know you are interested in their direct feedback — good, bad or indifferent.

The Objectives Conversation: Tell them you want to make sure you both are clear on your job objectives and how you can achieve them successfully.

The Career Development Conversation: Let them know you wish to set up a plan to increase your value to the company through training, skills development or new responsibilities. Emphasize how this could reflect well on them, by having a motivated, highly productive employee who could potentially be promoted or take on a greater role in the organization.

The Underlying Motivators Conversation: Talk about the value of knowing exactly what is important to you and how to help you perform at your best by "speaking" your motivation "language."

The Strengths Conversation: Discuss the concept of strengths and weaknesses and how helping employees to utilize their strengths more can result in lower employee turnover, greater productivity and higher job satisfaction. By identifying and using more of your strengths, you'll be of greater value to the company and a better staff member to them.

In my experience, the majority of managers will welcome this conversation. If they don't feel like they have the time to manage, they will probably be relieved that you're taking the responsibility on yourself and driving the process.

#3. Once you get their agreement to this framework, schedule monthly sessions and put it in their calendars.

Make sure you prepare for these conversations in advance and send them an agenda at least one week prior to the meeting to give them time to review the material. You might want to include questions or requests for them that you'd like to cover.

Be sure to document the conversations along with who is responsible for doing what between this and the next session. Send them an email asking for their understanding of what was discussed and what both you and they are accountable for.

Finally, follow up on these accountabilities. If they don't keep their end of the bargain, reiterate how important this is to you.

If you follow this structure, one of two things will happen. Either you will develop a great working relationship with your boss and will be able to help them help you with your present job and career path, or you'll find out definitively whether they can step up to the plate and be the manager you need them to be. And if you have been practicing the 5 *FOCUSed* Conversations with your staff, you may very well be ready to step into their shoes!

Bottom Line: Just Do It

The biggest challenge most people face when starting something new is to actually change their behavior. They think an approach is a great idea, but then they find it hard to change their ways. And this can be doubly or triply difficult if you as the manager are trying yet "another new technique to get more work out of us" (as some of your staff may be saying amongst themselves).

Change is hard, but it has to start somewhere, and that "somewhere" is you. I suggest that you take yourself through these *FOCUSed* Conversations before you try them on your staff. But even if you're unsure of your results and wary of trying this on your team, give it a shot. Remember the HR studies that show even negative attention from a manager is better than being ignored?[39] What's the worst that could happen if you dedicated time each month to sit down with your staff, found out what's on their minds, discovered more about their career plans, strengths and what motivates them, and then asked them for feedback and *listened* to them?

I have seen some great results from implementing the 5 *FOCUSed* Conversations in businesses and watched as employee engagement, job satisfaction and productivity skyrocketed — not only for staff but for managers as well. But *you* have to lead your team into this new way of communicating.

Remember Bob, the staff member back in Chapter 2? Let's imagine that when Bob first joined your team you'd been using the 5 *FOCUSed* Conversations with your staff for a year or so. Therefore, as soon as Bob walked into the department for the first time you gave him a firm handshake, a hearty "Welcome aboard!" — and a copy of this book. You told him to read it and be ready to go over the basics with you the following week, when you would schedule your first *FOCUSed* Conversation with him.

"We'll be having regular sessions for feedback between us both and going over your job objectives and making sure you have everything you need to achieve them," you tell Bob. "We'll also talk about your personal and professional objectives so we can make sure your life and your work are supporting each other. We'll get to know exactly what motivates you and how I can help you know when you're doing a great job, and finally, we'll figure out how to make the most of your strengths and mitigate your weaknesses.

"I hope that all of this will help you do a great job and enjoy your work here. But ultimately, it's up to you. This is just a framework; if you bring your 'A' game to this, I believe you'll be one of our department's superstars."

Bob was a little surprised but excited. He read *Mind Reading for Managers* over the weekend and walked in Monday ready to go. Over the months, you worked closely with Bob and you were really happy to see him fulfill his potential as he became one of your team's Critical People.

At the end of a year you called a meeting of the entire department. "We've exceeded our numbers and we are officially the most productive working group in the company," you announce. "This team has done wonders — and Bob, you've become a superstar. Your numbers pushed us over the top." Bob (who's motivated by External Praise) beams. You then present the entire team with the Chairman's Award, given to the best department in the organization.

As you look around, you see the faces of every member of your team glowing with pride — and engagement. All it took was a little mind reading on your part — and the commitment from both you and your team to honest, ongoing, *FOCUSed* Conversations.

Additional Resources

For more information on the 5 *FOCUSed* Conversations and other employee engagement tools for the Social Age, please visit http://igniteglobal.com.

To download the Conversation Starters and the *FOCUSed* Conversation Planner along with our free eBook, *Viva La Evolution: 5 C's to Attract, Engage and Retain Staff for the Social Age,* go to http://igniteglobal.com/mrfmbook/.

Ignite Global Corporate Programs

I gnite Global offers a series of consulting programs, live workshops and web-based training designed to help you to implement Social Age Engagement™ Solutions for greater employee engagement, retention and productivity.

Here is a sample of the Ignite Global curriculum.

Mind Reading for Managers: 5 *FOCUSed* Conversations for Greater Employee Engagement and Productivity

Interested in bringing the 5 *FOCUSed* Conversations for Greater Employee Engagement and Productivity to your organization? This live or web-based workshop (also available with a "Train the Trainer" program to enable you to deliver the program yourself) provides participants with a deep understanding of the material in this book. But it also equips managers and supervisors with additional Conversation and Coaching Skills as well as the Conversation Roadmap and accompanying exercises and tools to increase the effectiveness of conducting these conversations. This course may also be customized to incorporate your current performance review program.

Hiring for the Social Age: 3 Keys to Hire/Promote Top Talent in Today's Digitally Connected, Globally Oriented World

Bad hires cost organizations millions of dollars each year. Unfortunately, most managers have never been sufficiently trained on hiring well. Many resort to nothing more than gut feel when making this critical business decision — and often live to regret it. Additionally, hiring for the Social Age presents its own set of unique challenges. In our digitally connected, globally oriented world we must hire people to be more innovative, strategic and creative. We must hire problem solvers. And there is a very specific way to both attract and screen this top talent.

This live or web-based workshop (also available with a "Train the Trainer" program to enable you to deliver the program yourself) provides participants with a Framework and supporting Handbook of practical tools that are used to source, hire, evaluate, select, attract and onboard top talent, helping to ensure that each hire is the best hire. Participants will be thoroughly prepared to plan and conduct extremely robust, objective-based interviews to unlock critical information, which significantly increases hiring managers' success and the ability to attract and select the right candidates for building a great team.

Soar with Your Strengths: Strategies to Unleash Your Professional Superpowers and to Avoid Your Personal Kryptonite

What are your superpowers at work? We all have them. Those innate abilities not only make us unique but also can help to make us wildly successful. This short, fun and interactive workshop (delivered live or via the web) will help us not only discover our superpowers, but also to develop strategies to use them more often and more effectively, as well as strategies to avoid our own personal "kryptonite" — the weaknesses that keep us from performing at our best.

Secrets of a Great Career Revealed: 4 Steps to Career Management for High Potential Employees

© iStock/Hutlon Archive

Why should you help your high potential employees manage their careers better? Because studies show it is one of the most effective and least costly employee engagement and retention strategies a company can offer.

This live workshop focuses on assisting your Critical People to see a clear career path within your organization. They will learn to set and reach both personal and professional goals, understand and leverage their strengths and develop the resilience needed stay the course during trying times. And this is accomplished at a fraction of the cost of traditional executive coaching!

Additional Workshops and Consulting Programs can be found at

http://IgniteGlobal.com

Info@IgniteGlobal.com
US: (512) 333-4587
Australia: 1300 667 861

About the Author

© Ross Dalton

An international expert on Human Resources in the Social Age, Kim Seeling Smith disrupts outdated, Industrial Age methods and mindsets and replaces them with Social Age Engagement™ Solutions.

Through her company, Ignite Global, Kim helps organizations build healthy work environments and increase employee engagement and productivity in our 21st century, digitally connected, globally oriented world through programs built around the 5 C's Framework.

Originally trained as a CPA and Management Consultant with KPMG, Kim subsequently spent 15 years working as an international recruiter, giving her a front-row seat from which to study why some companies are great at attracting and engaging staff while others constantly struggle with turnover.

Kim was invited to judge the 2012, 2013 & 2014 Australian HR Awards and 2014 Middle East HR Excellence Awards and was appointed as a Subject Matter Expert to advise a U.S.-based, multi-national financial services firm's global Senior Leadership Project Team on increasing employee engagement within the company.

She is a frequent presenter for business, trade organization and corporate conferences as well as for the American Society of Human Resource Management (SHRM), the Australian Human Resources Institute (AHRI), and Australia and Singapore's HR Summit Series, amongst others. She is regularly featured in business trade journals all over the world. Kim is a also a co-author, along with Brian Tracy, of *101 Great Ways to Enhance Your Career.*

Born in the United States, Kim has spent over a decade living and working in Australia, New Zealand and Asia. Living her life long dream of "following the sun," Kim now splits her time between the U.S. and Australia.

To contact Kim, visit http://IgniteGlobal.com.

Endnotes

1   Mitra Toosi, "Labor Force Projections to 2020: A More Slowly Growing Workforce,"
    Monthly Labor Review, January 2012, 43-64, http://www.bls.gov/opub/mlr/2012/01/
    art3full.pdf

2   "The Organizational Challenges of Global Trends: A McKinsey Global Survey," The
    McKinsey Quarterly, December 2007, mckinseyquarterly.com. Cited in Matthew
    Guthridge, Asmus B. Komm, and Emily Lawson, "Making Talent a Strategic Priority,"
    The McKinsey Quarterly, No. 1, 2008, http://www.leadway.org/PDF/Making%20tal-
    ent%20a%20strategic%20priority.pdf.

3   Charles Fishman, an interview with Ed Michaels, "The War for Talent," *Fast Company*,
    July 31, 1998, http://www.fastcompany.com/34512/war-talent.

4   David G. Allen, Ph.D. *Retaining Talent: A Guide To Analyzing And Managing Employee
    Turnover*. SHRM Foundation's Effective Practice Guidelines Series. SHRM Founda-
    tion, 2008, p. 3. http://www.shrm.org/about/foundation/research/documents/retain-
    ing%20talent-%20final.pdf.

5   Kevin A. Hassett and Robert J. Shapiro. *What Ideas are Worth: The Value of Intellectual
    Capital and Intangible Assets in the American Economy*. White paper, Sonecon, 2011,
    http://www.sonecon.com/docs/studies/Value_of_Intellectual_Capital_in_American_
    Economy.pdf

6   *Global Human Capital Trends 2014: Engaging the 21st-Century Workforce*. A report
    by Deloitte Consulting LLP and Bersin by Deloitte. Deloitte Development LLC,
    2014, pp. 7-8, http://www.deloitte.com/assets/Dcom-Namibia/GlobalHumanCapital-
    Trends2014_030714.pdf.

7   *State of the Global Workplace: Employee Engagement Insights for Business Leaders
    Worldwide*. Gallup, Inc., 2013. State of the Global Workplace Report 2013.pdf,
    downloaded from http://www.gallup.com/strategicconsulting/164735/state-global-
    workplace.aspx. Unless otherwise cited, all employee engagement statistics come
    from the 2013 report. Since The Gallup Organization began monitoring employee
    engagement in the 1990s, they have surveyed 25 million employees in 195 countries
    and 70 languages.

[8]   Mary Lorenz, "How Much Does a Bad Employee Cost the Boss?" *Careerbuilder.com,* January 27, 2012, http://www.careerbuilder.com/article/cb-2819-leadership-management-how-much-does-a-bad-employee-cost-the-boss/.

[9]   *State of the Global Workplace: Employee Engagement Insights for Business Leaders Worldwide,* p. 83.

[10] *State of the Global Workplace: Employee Engagement Insights for Business Leaders Worldwide,* p. 78.

[11] E. Chambers, M. Foulon, H. Handfield-Jones, S. Hankin, and E. Michaels. *The War for Talent,* The McKinsey Quarterly 1998, No. 3, www.northstarhr.com/pdf/documents/the_war_for_talent.pdf.

[12] Alan Murray, "The End of Management," *Wall Street Journal,* Aug. 21, 2010, http://online.wsj.com/news/articles/SB10001424052748704476104575439723695579664.

[13] See http://www.selfdeterminationtheory.org/.

[14] This quote comes from Daniel Pink's 2009 talk at TEDGlobal, https://www.ted.com/talks/dan_pink_on_motivation/transcript.

[15] *Clear Direction in a Complex World: How Top Companies Create Clarity, Confidence and Community to Build Sustainable Performance.* A 2011-2012 Change and Communication ROI Study Report, TW-NA-2011-19860. Towers Watson, 2011, p. 3, http://www.distinction-services.com/resources/videoblog/Towers-Watson-2012%20ROI%20on%20Comm.pdf.

[16] https://www.gallupstrengthscenter.com/.

[17] Marcus Buckingham and Donald O. Clifton, Now, *Discover Your Strengths* (New York: Free Press, 2001), pp. 50-53.

[18] Susan Sorenson, "How Employees' Strengths Make Your Company Stronger," *Gallup Business Journal,* February 20, 2014, http://businessjournal.gallup.com/content/167462/employees-strengths-company-stronger.aspx.

[19] Benson Smith and Tony Rutigilano, *Discover Your Sales Strengths: How the World's Greatest Salespeople Develop Winning Careers* (New York: Business Plus, 2003), pp. 179-180.

[20] Leslie Allan, "Gallup Study: Impact of Manager Feedback on Employee Engagement," HR Management Blog, Toolbox.com, February 22, 2011, http://hr.toolbox.com/blogs/people-at-work/gallup-study-impact-of-manager-feedback-on-employee-engagement-43509. Also Brian Brim and Jim Asplund, "Driving Engagement by Focusing on Strengths," *Gallup Business Journal*, November 12, 2009, http://businessjournal.gallup.com/content/124214/driving-engagement-focusing-strengths.aspx.

21 Marcial Losada and Emily Heaphy, "The Role of Positivity and Connectivity in the Performance of Business Teams: A Nonlinear Dynamics Model," *American Behavioral Scientist* 47 (2004), 740-765, http://www.factorhappiness.at/downloads/quellen/S8_Losada.pdf

[22] Alexander Kjerulf, "The Top 5 Ways Not to Praise People at Work," *The Chief Happiness Officer Blog*, September 12, 2012, http://positivesharing.com/2012/09/the-top-5-ways-not-to-praise-people-at-work/.

[23] "SHRM Presentation" by The Wynhurst Group, April 2007. Cited in Thomas J. Purcell, "3 Topics Every Job Candidate Should Bring Up During an Interview," May 2, 2012, http://ezinearticles.com/?3-Topics-Every-Job-Candidate-Should-Bring-Up-During-an-Interview&id=7037972

[24] Study reported by Jacqueline Smith, "Why Your Top Talent is Leaving in 2014, and What It'll Take to Retain Them," *Forbes online*, January 24, 2014, http://www.forbes.com/sites/jacquelynsmith/2014/01/24/why-your-top-talent-is-leaving-in-2014-and-what-itll-take-to-retain-them/. Here are the reasons people say they are thinking about leaving their current jobs: Concerns over salary (66 percent); don't feel valued (65 percent); dissatisfied with advancement opportunities at current company (45 percent); dissatisfied with work/life balance (39 percent); feel underemployed (39 percent); highly stressed (39 percent); feel they were overlooked for a promotion (36 percent); been at their companies for two years or less (35 percent); and didn't receive a pay increase in 2013 (28 percent).

[25] G.E.P. Box and N.R. Draper, *Empirical Model-Building and Response Surfaces* (New York: John Wiley & Sons, 1987), p. 424.

[26] Daniel H. Pink, *Drive: The Surprising Truth About What Motivates Us* (New York: Riverhead, 2009).

[27] Abraham H. Maslow, "A theory of human motivation," *Psychological Review*, 50, no. 4 (1943), 370–96.

[28] Frederick Herzberg, "The Motivation-Hygiene Concept and Problems of Manpower," *Personnel Administrator* 27 (January–February 1964), pp. 3–7.

[29] These studies form the basis of the book, *Drive* (see endnote 26).

30 Mark Milian, "How a YouTube Exec Built an Army With Google's '20 Percent Time,'" *Bloomberg Google Tech Blog*, October 17, 2012, http://go.bloomberg.com/tech-blog/2012-10-17-how-a-youtube-exec-built-an-army-with-googles-20-percent-time.

31 See http://solutions.3m.com/innovation/en_US/stories/time-to-think.

32 Peter Drucker, *Managing for the Future: The 1990s and Beyond* (New York: Dutton Adult, 1992), p. 139.

33 The books focused on strengths and based on research from the Gallup Organization include Donald O. Clifton and Paula Nelson, *Soar With Your Strengths: A Simple Yet Revolutionary Philosophy of Business and Management* (New York: Dell, 1995); Marcus Buckingham and Curt Coffman, *First, Break All the Rules: What the World's Greatest Managers Do Differently* (New York: Simon & Schuster, 1999); Buckingham and Donald O. Clifton, *Now, Discover Your Strengths* (New York: Free Press, 2001); Tom Rath, *StrengthsFinder 2.0* (New York: Gallup Press, 2007); Rath and Barry Conchie, *Strengths Based Leadership: Great Leaders, Teams, and Why People Follow Them* (New York: Gallup Press, 2009).

34 Rath and Conchie, *Strengths Based Leadership*, p. 2.

35 Clifton and Nelson, *Soar With Your Strengths*, p. 12-13.

36 *Why Strengths? The Evidence.* White paper, CAPP 2010, http://www.cappeu.com/Portals/3/Files/Why_Strengths_The_Evidence.pdf

37 "The Realize 4M Model," http://www.cappeu.com/Realise2/TheRealise24MModel.aspx

38 Rath, *StrengthsFinder 2.0*, p. 35.

39 Leslie Allan, "Gallup Study: Impact of Manager Feedback on Employee Engagement," *HR Toolbox blog*, February 22, 2011, http://hr.toolbox.com/blogs/people-at-work/gallup-study-impact-of-manager-feedback-on-employee-engagement-43509.

Made in the USA
Middletown, DE
14 November 2019